ONLINE EXPLORATIONS IN WORLD HISTORY

CORRELATION GUIDE WITH ACCESS CODE

for

World History

William J. Duiker

Jackson J. Spielvogel

THOMSON
WADSWORTH™

Australia • Canada • Mexico • Singapore • Spain • United Kingdom • United States

Printed in Canada
1 2 3 4 5 6 7 07 06 05 04

Printer: Webcom

0-534-62718-8

For more information about our products, contact us at:
Thomson Learning Academic Resource Center
1-800-423-0563

For permission to use material from this text or product, submit a request online at
http://www.thomsonrights.com
Any additional questions about permissions can be submitted at
thomsonrights@thomson.com

Thomson Wadsworth
10 Davis Drive
Belmont, CA 94002-3098
USA

Asia
Thomson Learning
5 Shenton Way #01-01
UIC Building
Singapore 068808

Australia/New Zealand
Thomson Learning
102 Dodds Street
Southbank, Victoria 3006
Australia

Canada
Nelson
1120 Birchmount Road
Toronto, Ontario M1K 5G4
Canada

Europe/Middle East/South Africa
Thomson Learning
High Holborn House
50/51 Bedford Row
London WC1R 4LR
United Kingdom

Latin America
Thomson Learning
Seneca, 53
Colonia Polanco
11560 Mexico D.F.
Mexico

Spain/Portugal
Paraninfo
Calle/Magallanes, 25
28015 Madrid, Spain

HistoryNow

ONLINE EXPLORATIONS IN WORLD HISTORY CORRELATION GUIDE WITH ACCESS CODE FOR

World History

WILLIAM J DUIKER * JACKSON J. SPIELVOGEL

CHAPTER 1:	**THE FIRST CIVILIZATIONS: THE PEOPLES OF WESTERN ASIA AND EGYPT**
Modules:	Origins of Western Civilization: Mesopotamia and Egypt, 3000 - 1200 B.C.E.
CHAPTER 2:	**ANCIENT INDIA**
Modules:	No modules for this chapter
CHAPTER 3:	**CHINA IN ANTIQUITY**
Modules:	No modules for this chapter
CHAPTER 4:	**THE CIVILIZATION OF THE GREEKS**
Modules:	Ancient Greek and Roman Art and Architecture, ca 550 .C.E. - 330 C.E.
CHAPTER 5:	**THE WORLD OF THE ROMANS**
Modules:	Ancient Greek and Roman Art and Architecture, ca 550 .C.E. - 330 C.E.
CHAPTER 6:	**THE NEW WORLD**
Modules:	No modules for this chapter
CHAPTER 7:	**THE WORLDS OF ISLAM AND BYZANTIUM**
Modules:	No modules for this chapter
CHAPTER 8:	**EARLY CIVILIZATIONS IN AFRICA**
Modules:	No modules for this chapter

CHAPTER 9:	**THE EXPANSION OF CIVILIZATION IN SOUTHERN ASIA**
Modules:	No modules for this chapter
CHAPTER 10:	**FROM THE TANG TO THE MONGOLS: THE FLOWERING OF TRADITIONAL CHINA**
Modules:	No modules for this chapter
CHAPTER 11:	**THE EAST ASIAN RIMLANDS: EARLY JAPAN, KOREA, AND VIETNAM**
Modules:	No modules for this chapter
CHAPTER 12:	**THE MAKING OF EUROPE IN THE MIDDLE AGES**
Modules:	Medieval Art and Architecture, ca. 476 C.E. - 1453 C.E.
	A Year in the Life of a Medieval Peasant Family
CHAPTER 13:	**RENEWAL, REFORM, AND STATE BUILDING IN EUROPE**
Modules:	Empire: Politics, Conquest, and Dissolution (1500-2000)
	The Silver Trade and the World Economy (1500-1700)
	Exploring a Renaissance Painting
	Warfare in Early Modern Europe: 1494 – 1648
CHAPTER 14:	**NEW ENCOUNTERS: THE CREATION OF A WORLD MARKET**
Modules:	Empire: Politics, Conquest, and Dissolution (1500-2000)
	The Silver Trade and the World Economy (1500-1700)
	God, Gold and Glory: Columbus and the Age of Exploration, 1413 - 1776

CHAPTER 15: **THE MUSLIM EMPIRES**

Modules: Empire: Politics, Conquest, and Dissolution (1500-2000)

CHAPTER 16: **THE EAST ASIAN WORLD**

Modules: Empire: Politics, Conquest, and Dissolution (1500-2000)

CHAPTER 17: **THE WEST ON THE EVE OF A NEW WORLD ORDER**

Modules: Empire: Politics, Conquest, and Dissolution (1500-2000)

The French Revolution: The Summer of 1789 and the Origins of the French Revolution

The Order of the Day - Terror in the French Revolution, 1792 – 1794

The Wars of the French Revolution, 1792 – 1799

Napoleonic Europe

CHAPTER 18: **THE BEGINNINGS OF MODERNIZATION: INDUSTRIALIZATION AND NATIONALISM, 1800-1870**

Modules: Industrialization in World History

Women at Work: Female Labor in World History (1700-1850)

World Migration (1840-1920)

Nation Building, 1848 - 1870: Italy, Germany and Comparative Examples

The Revolutions of 1848

Unification of Italy

Unification of Germany

CHAPTER 19: **THE EMERGENCE OF MASS SOCIETY IN THE WESTERN WORLD**

Modules: World Migration (1840-1920)

An Industrial Life: Isambard Kingdom Brunel, 1806 – 1859

Aspects of Modernism: The Visual Arts, 1863 – 1939

CHAPTER 20: **THE HIGH TIDE OF IMPERIALISM**

Modules: Empire: Politics, Conquest, and Dissolution (1500-2000)

World Migration (1840-1920)

European Imperialism 1880 - 1900: Theory, Practice, Discourse

CHAPTER 21: **SHADOWS OVER THE PACIFIC: EAST ASIA UNDER CHALLENGE**

Modules: Empire: Politics, Conquest, and Dissolution (1500-2000)

World Migration (1840-1920)

Industrialization in World History

World Migration (1840-1920)

CHAPTER 22: **THE BEGINNING OF THE TWENTIETH CENTURY CRISIS: WAR AND REVOLUTION**

Modules: The Origins of World War I

War and Conflict in the 20th Century

International Organizations in the 20th Century

Empire: Politics, Conquest, and Dissolution (1500-2000)

CHAPTER 23: **NATIONALISM, REVOLUTION, AND DICTATORSHIP: AFRICA, ASIA, AND LATIN AMERICA FROM 1919 TO 1939**

Modules: Empire: Politics, Conquest, and Dissolution (1500-2000)

War and Conflict in the 20th Century

"A New World Arisen": Russia's Revolutions, 1900 - 1924

CHAPTER 24: **THE CRISIS DEEPENS: WORLD WAR II**

Modules: Empire: Politics, Conquest, and Dissolution (1500-2000)

International Organizations in the 20th Century

War and Conflict in the 20th Century

CHAPTER 25: **IN THE GRIP OF THE COLD WAR: THE BREAKDOWN OF THE YALTA SYSTEM**

Modules: Empire: Politics, Conquest, and Dissolution (1500-2000)

War and Conflict in the 20th Century

International Organizations in the 20th Century

Reconstructing Capitalist Europe, 1945-1960: The Marshall Plan

CHAPTER 26: **BRAVE NEW WORLD: COMMUNISM ON TRIAL**

Modules: War and Conflict in the 20th Century

CHAPTER 27: **EUROPE AND THE WESTERN HEMISPHERE SINCE 1945**

Modules: International Organizations in the 20th Century

CHAPTER 28:	**CHALLENGES OF NATION BUILDING IN AFRICA AND THE MIDDLE EAST**
Modules:	Ties That Bind: Family in 20th Century World History Empire: Politics, Conquest, and Dissolution (1500-2000) War and Conflict in the 20th Century
CHAPTER 29:	**TOWARD THE PACIFIC CENTURY?**
Modules:	Empire: Politics, Conquest, and Dissolution (1500-2000) War and Conflict in the 20th Century

HistoryNow

HistoryNow's 29 robust interactive online explorations of World History bring the past to life through seamless integration of text and context, interactive maps and timelines, images and photos, readings and primary source documents, related artwork and visual data, and so much more! These self-contained, easy-to-navigate modules—framed by proven pedagogy—encourage students to interrogate the material and engage in new ways of thinking.

To access these modules go to our HistoryNow Website for World History at http://historynow.wadsworth.com/world/ and type in the access code that is printed on the card at the front of this booklet.

FEATURES WITHIN HISTORYNOW'S INTERACTIVE MODULES

- **Context:** A brief overview of the interactive module and its key learning objectives.

- **Interactive module:** The 30-90 minute learning experience covering a key historical topic.

    - **Navigating an interactive module:** Every HistoryNow interactive module can be navigated from the module's home page by clicking on any of the sections displayed on the center screen, or from anywhere in the module by clicking on the top section titles, which will then show drop-down menus indicating components of each section. Once you have begun working through the module, you can either click the forward arrow or back arrow (found at the lower right and left of the screen) or go to the top and navigate component by component within any given section. You will find that upon visiting a component within a section, an "X" will appear next to the title of that section in the drop-down menu (and will remain there during that particular session).

- **Historical Documents:** Primary and secondary readings contained within the interactive module that can be easily printed by right-clicking on any given document and selecting Print.

- **Glossary Terms:** Definitions of key terms and figures contained within the interactive module.

- **Questions:** This folder contains 4-6 short answer questions that the student should be able to answer upon completing the interactive module.

Click on various icons indicating opportunities for additional information or exploration.

 Map

 Photograph

 Related Text

 Enlarge Image

 Context

 Question

 Related Visual Data

HistoryNow: Online Explorations in World History

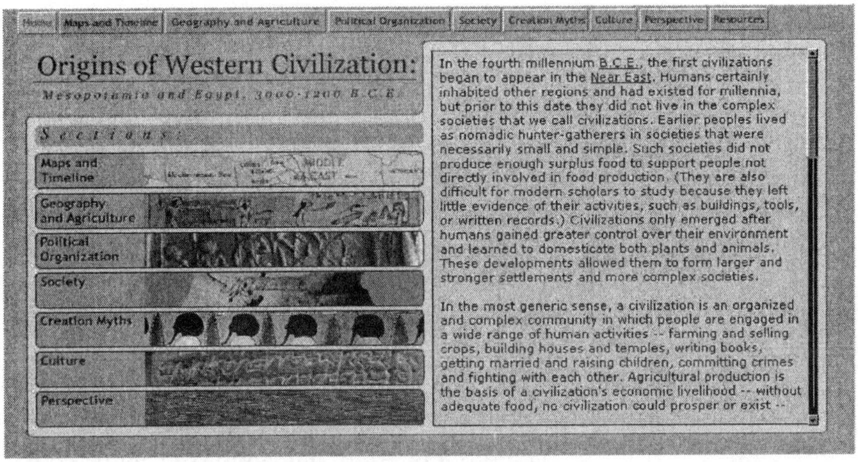

Origins of Western Civilization: Mesopotamia and Egypt, 3000 - 1200 B.C.E.

This module compares the Bronze Age societies of Mesopotamia and Egypt. It examines the geography, agriculture, economy, social structure, religion, and cultural achievements of each society, taking particular note of the similarities and differences between the two societies.

Readings:

- Sumerian Farmer's Almanac, ca. 1700 B.C.E.
- The Baal Myth from Ugarit, retold by Paul Brassey
- Mesopotamian Contracts, ca. 2300-2000 B.C.E.
- Enuma Elish
- Gilgamesh, Tablets 1–8, Anonymous, translated by William Ellery Leonard
- Hammurabi's Code of Laws, translated by L. W. King
- The Histories, Book 2, chapters 5-10, 19, 26, 35-36, Herodotus
- Egyptian Love Poetry, ca. 2000-1100 B.C.E.
- Memphite Theology of Creation, translated by John A. Wilson
- The Precepts of Ptah-Hotep, ca. 2200 B.C.E.
- Pyramid Texts, excerpts
- The Legend of Sargon of Akkadia, ca. 2300 B.C.E.

- Description of Egyptian Weather from A History of the Ancient Egyptians (1911), pp. 10–11, James Henry Breasted

SECTION QUESTIONS

- Geography and Agriculture
    1. How were the geographies of ancient Mesopotamia and Egypt similar? Different?
    2. In what ways was Mesopotamian agriculture similar to that of Egypt? How was it different?
    3. Based on the similarities and differences between the geographies of Mesopotamia and Egypt, how would you expect the worldviews of residents of each society to be similar? Different?

- Political Organization
    1. What challenges did political leaders in Mesopotamia face? What could they do in such situations?
    2. What are some of the primary differences between Egyptian and Mesopotamia political organization? What may have caused these differences?

- Society
    1. How might the daily lives of Mesopotamian and Egyptian commoners been similar? Different?
    2. Why might ancient Mesopotamians and Egyptians have had such different views of the afterlife?

- Creation Myths
    1. What common questions do pre-modern creation myths seek to answer?
    2. In what ways are Egyptian and Sumerian creation myths similar? Different? What might account for the differences?

- Culture
    1. What similar cultural developments emerged in Egypt and Mesopotamia? Why might these similarities have existed?
    2. How did social and economic conditions influence the particular cultural developments that emerged (or didn't emerge) in Mesopotamia and Egypt?

MODULE LEVEL QUESTIONS

1. How did the geographical conditions of Mesopotamia and Egypt shape the societies that emerged in each place?
2. In what ways are Egyptian and Sumerian creation myths similar? Different?
3. What are some of the primary differences between Egyptian and Mesopotamian political organization?
4. What similar cultural developments emerged in Egypt and Mesopotamia?

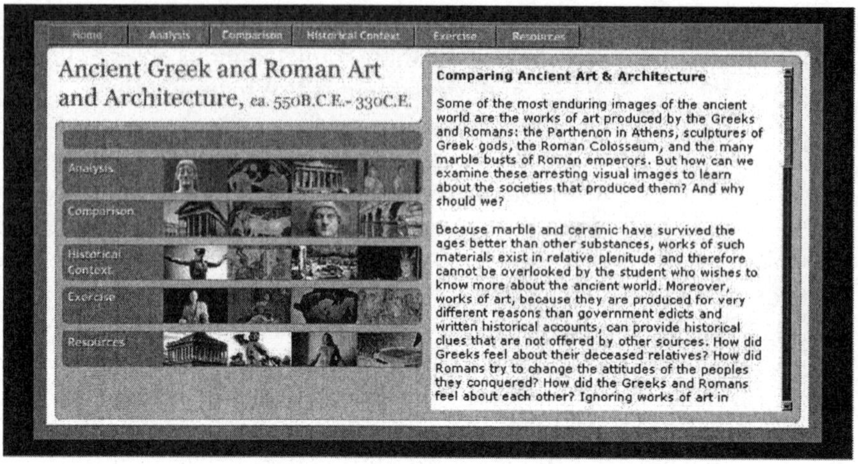

ANCIENT GREEK AND ROMAN ART AND ARCHITECTURE, CA 550 C.E. - 330 C.E.

This module provides an overview of some of the major styles and media of ancient art via select works. Through the accompanying analytical essays, students are exposed to how historians and art historians use works of art as a historical source. All images are placed in their historical context via a timeline of events and developments.

READINGS:

- Athenian Constitution, 20-22, Aristotle
- Histories, Books 6 and 7, Herodotus
- The Iliad, chapter 1 (ca. 800 B.C.E.), Homer, translated by Samuel Butler
- The History of Rome, Book I, Livy
- Symposium, Plato
- Life of Alexander, Plutarch
- Life of Caesar, Plutarch
- History of the Peloponnesian War, Book 2, ch. 34–46, Thucydides
- The Aeneid, Book I, Virgil

Section Questions

- Exercise 1
    1. When and where might this work have been created? What suggests that time and place?
    2. What are the dominant characteristics of this work? What do they suggest about the artist's intent?
    3. How does this work compare to some of the other sculptures in this module? How is it similar? Different? What does this tell you about this work?

- Exercise 2
    1. When and where might this work have been created? What suggests that time and place?
    2. What are the dominant characteristics of this work? What do they suggest about that society's technological and financial resources?
    3. What might have been the original purpose of this structure? What suggests that? How might that purpose have changed over time?

Module Level Questions

1. What artistic styles are characteristic of Classical Greek art? What connection might there be between such style and Greek society?
2. What artistic styles are characteristic of Hellenistic art? What connection might there be between such style and Hellenistic society?
3. Some claim that Roman society did not produce any original art but only borrowed from the Greeks. To what extent is this valid? Invalid?
4. What sort of building projects did Romans tend to undertake? How does this compare with the projects undertaken by Greek and Hellenistic architects?

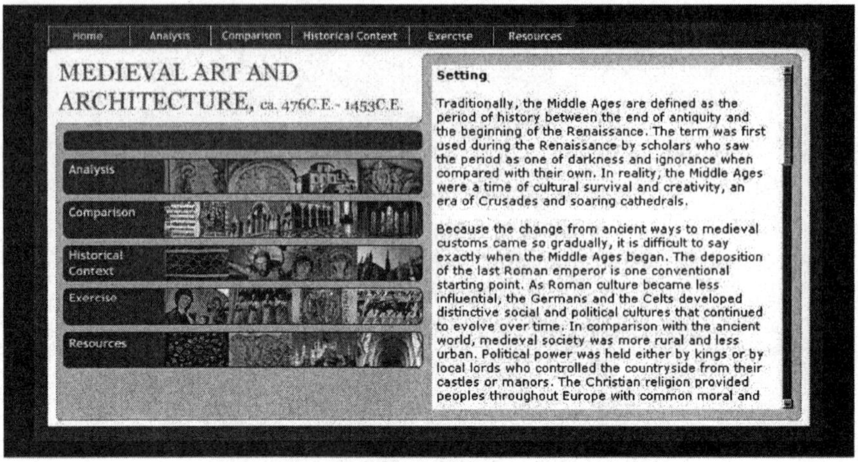

MEDIEVAL ART AND ARCHITECTURE CA. 476 C.E. - 1453 C.E. This module provides an overview of some of the major styles and media of medieval art via a select sampling of works. Through the accompanying analytical essays, students are exposed to the ways that historians and art historians use artwork as a historical source. All images are placed in their historical context via a timeline of events and developments.

READINGS:

- Jean Froissart chronicles the Hundred Years' War (1370-1400), The Battle of Crécy
- The Anglo-Saxon Chronicle, Entry for 1066
- Assize of Clarendon, 1166
- The Ecclesiastical History of the English Nation, Book One, ch. 23-26, The Venerable Bede
- Rule of Saint Benedict, Sixth Century
- The Decameron: Introduction, Giovanni Boccaccio
- Clericis Laicos, 1296
- Charter of Cluny, 910
- The Divine Comedy: Inferno, Cantos 1-5, Dante Alighieri
- The Divine Comedy: Paradiso, Canto 33, Dante Alighieri
- Life of Charlemagne, Ch. 1–4, 15–31, Einhard
- Life of Saint Francis of Assisi, Ch. 1–3, 7, 13, Saint Bonaventure
- Rule of Saint Francis of Assisi, 1223
- Dictatus Papae (The Dictates of the Pope), ca. 1075, attributed to Pope Gregory VII

- Letter of Louis IX to his son
- Magna Carta (Great Charter)
- Secret History, Book 8, Procopius
- Account of Pope Urban II's speech at Clermont, 1095, Robert the Monk

SECTION QUESTIONS

- Exercise 1
  1. What style of architecture dominates this church? What elements suggest that? What would be the impact of this architectural style on someone entering to worship?
  2. What architectural features are visible from the outside of the church? What does this suggest about the building techniques used and the goals of the builders?
  3. Was this church more likely intended to serve a closed monastic community or a large public community?
  4. What can you infer about the society that devoted its energy and resources to creating buildings such as this?

- Exercise 2
  1. What was the intended purpose of this work? What suggests that?
  2. What does the nature of this work suggest about the value that the artist and the commissioner placed on it? What might have caused it?
  3. What might one say about the representation of the figures here? What does that suggest about the artist's skill or the values of the community he served?

MODULE LEVEL QUESTIONS

1. Medieval societies devoted tremendous energy and resources to building various kinds of churches. What can those churches tell us about those societies?
2. How do some of the churches built in the central and high Middle Ages reflect the ideals of the monastic reform movement?
3. How did Gothic churches try to convey the majesty of God?
4. Over the course of the Middle Ages, book illustration changed in both size and content. What do these changes suggest about the changes in literacy and spiritual devotion?

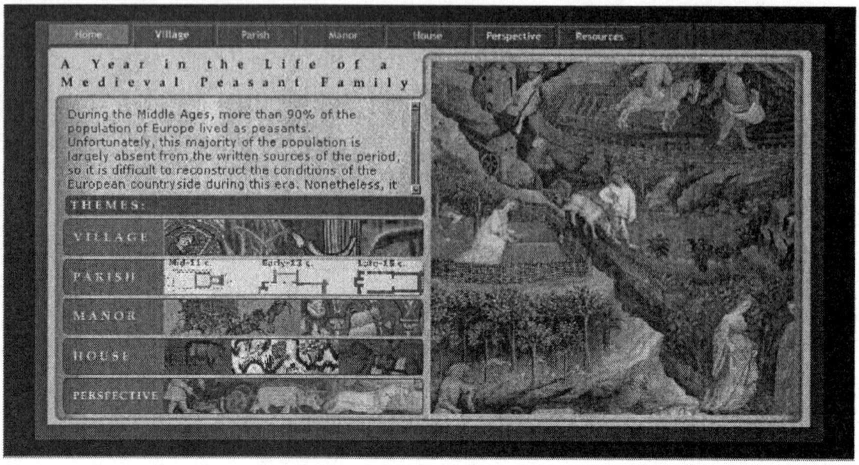

A YEAR IN THE LIFE OF A MEDIEVAL PEASANT FAMILY

This module gives the student the opportunity to explore a year in the life of a medieval peasant family. In addition to the seasonal tasks, the module presents some of the limitations of, and innovations in, medieval agricultural production.

READINGS:

- Asnapium, ca. 800, An Inventory of One of Charlemagne's Estates
- The Dialogue Between Master & Disciple: On Laborers, ca. 1000
- Manorial Management and Organization, ca. 1270s, Plowing and Cultivating
- Manorial Management and Organization, ca. 1270s, Animal Husbandry
- Description of Manor House, 1265
- Polyptyque de Villeneuve St. Georeges, early 9th century, Abbot Irminon
- Survey of Somersham, 1222
- Tithable Products of the Land, ca. 1115, from Leges Edwardis Confessoris

SECTION QUESTIONS

- Village
    1. What innovations in the Middle Ages may have improved agricultural productivity? What were some of the limitations of those innovations?
    2. What factor(s) might have caused or prevented a village from having a particularly productive or unproductive year?
    3. What aspects of medieval agricultural production continue to shape the modern world?
    4. What might an individual peasant or group of peasants have done to try to improve the productivity or the land or their own prosperity?
- Parish
    1. In what ways did the Church shape the world of medieval peasants?
    2. How might a medieval peasant's view of the Church's role in his life compare to a bishop or abbot's view of that role?
    3. How might a medieval peasant's Christian worship compare to modern ideas of the role of religion in a person's life?
- Manor
    1. How did the manor shape the world and daily activities of medieval peasants?
    2. Some modern thinkers assert that manorialism was a particularly unjust and burdensome economic system. What factors support that position? What factors do not? In what ways was the manor well suited to the agricultural conditions of the Middle Ages?
    3. What might a manorial lord or his deputies have done to make things more difficult for the peasants living on the manor? To ease their burden?

- House
    1. What would it have been like to live in the home of a medieval peasant?
    2. How could a well-run peasant home contribute to the prosperity of a medieval peasant family? How might a poorly run home imperil that prosperity?
    3. How did different family members contribute to the household economy? What might a family do in the absence of certain members, or if other family members joined the household?

MODULE LEVEL QUESTIONS

1. What innovations in the Middle Ages may have improved agricultural productivity?
2. What were the main characteristics of Christian worship in the peasant village?
3. How did the institution of the manor shape the world and daily activities of medieval peasants?
4. How could a well-run peasant home contribute to the prosperity of a medieval peasant family?

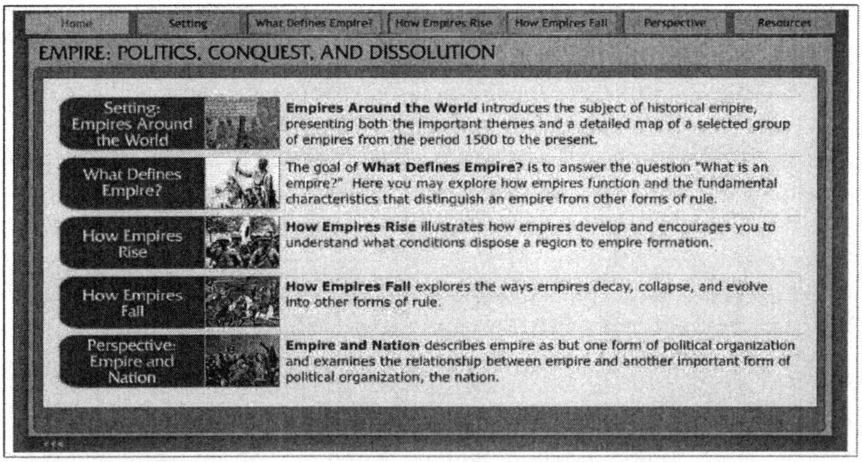

EMPIRE: POLITICS, CONQUEST, AND DISSOLUTION (1500-2000)
This module explores the historical role of empire in world history by investigating a large sampling of empires and uncovering factors that help students understand what an empire is and how it functions as a distinct form of human political organization. The module includes detailed studies of empires in Africa, East Asia, the Middle East, and North America.

READINGS:

- Abu'l Fazl, Akbarnama (1601)
- James Barbot, A Voyage to the New Calabar River (1699)
- Simón Bolívar, The Jamaica Letter (1815)
- Bartolomé de Las Casas, In Defense of the Indians (1550)
- Encomienda Regulations in Paraguay (1556)
- Leo Africanus, *The History and Description of Africa*, excerpts
- *The Epic of Askia Mohammed,* Transcription of an Oral History, Recounted by Nouhou Malio
- Al-Sa'di's Ta'rikh al-Soudan The Reign of Sunni 'Ali
- An Account of the Sa'dian Conquest of Songhay by an Anonymous Spaniard
- John L. O'Sullivan, Annexation (1845)
- The Greater East Asia Co-Prosperity Sphere (1940), Japanese Foreign Minister Arita
- A Typical African Blank Treaty, 1880's
- President Grover Cleveland's Message, December 18, 1893

- The Future Policy of Japan (Summary of Articles in "Jiji Shimpo" in June and July, 1895.) Count Tadasu Hayashi
- Treaty and Additional Agreement between China and Japan Respecting Manchuria, Peking, 22nd December, 1905
- *Under the Black Umbrella: Voices from Colonial Korea, 1901-1945*, excerpts, Hildegarde S. Kang
- Dawn of a New Asia from *The Goal of Japanese Expansion* Tatsuo Kawai
- The White Man's Burden (1899) Rudyard Kipling
- On Tactics Against Japanese Imperialism Report to Conference of Party Activists, December 27, 1935, Mao Zedong
- Japan as Coloniser, Inazo Nitobé
- The White Disaster, Okakura-Kakuzo
- The Roosevelt Corollary to the Monroe Doctrine, Theodore Roosevelt's Annual Message to Congress, 6 December 1904
- *Japan's Essential Purposes,* From an address before the Army and Navy Club and the Japan-America Society, at Chicago, May 21, 1934 Hirosi Saito
- Twenty-One Demands, Japanese Treaty with China, 1915
- Demand for Algerian Independence, 1960, Ferhat Abbas, Premier of the Provisional Government of the Algerian Republic
- Conversations between Tsar Nicholas I of Russia and Sir George Hamilton Seymour, the British Minister to Russia, 1853
- Proclamation of Revolt, 24 February 1821, Alexander Ypsilantis
- The Treaty of Kutchuk Kainardji, 21 July 1774
- "Turkey," from *The Eastern Question* Karl Marx
- Written Evidence Submitted to the Defence Committee by Professor Michael MccGwire Jan. 9, 1998 House of Commons, To Find a Role
- The Black Man's Burden (1920), Edmund D. Morel
- Program of the Society of National Defense, 1911
- Shooting an Elephant, George Orwell
- The Unilateral Declaration of Independence of Rhodesia
- Whether the Maintenance of An Army of Janissaries according to the Original Institution, be now agreeable to the Rules of Polity amongst the Turks. Paul Rycaut
- Second Report, Dependent Territories Review: Interim Report

- Excerpts from U.S. Senate Debates on Imperialism, 1900
- The Turkish Letters (excerpt), Ogier Ghiselin de Busbecq, Imperial Ambassador to Constantinople
- The Young Turks: Proclamation for the Ottoman Empire, 1908
- Nzinga Mbemba (Afonso I), Letters to the King of Portugal (1526)
- The National Emblem, 1898, William Jennings Bryan
- The Acquisition of Colonies, 1909, Archibald Cary Coolidge
- Hawaii, Complaint Against the United States of America to the United Nations, July 5, 2001
- The Philippine Problem: A Proposition for a Solution (1901), Sixto Lopez
- *The Influence of Sea Power Upon History, 1660-1783*, excerpts, Captain A.T. Mahan, D.C.L., LL.D.
- The Monroe Doctrine, December 2, 1823
- The Anglo-Saxon and the World's Future, Josiah Strong
- The Rough Riders, Ch. 3: General Young's Fight at Las Guasimas, Theodore Roosevelt
- The Significance of the Frontier in American History, Frederick Jackson Turner
- "To a Person Sitting in Darkness," 1901, Mark Twain
- Juan Ginés de Sepúlveda, Democrates Secundus, or The Just Causes of War Against the Indians (1547)

SECTION QUESTIONS

- Settings
    1. The Setting covers an extensive list of empires. Can you think of other empires that might also have appeared on this list? When might they have been considered "expanding" or in "decline"? What regions could be considered the "home" or "outer" portion of these empires?
    2. Is it possible for any form of government (such as a monarchy or a republic) to become an empire? Is any one form more likely to develop into an empire than another?
- What defines Empire?
    1. Empires function on many different levels at once. Which of these functions are the most significant? Are some functions absolutely essential while others are only tangential?

2. In the history of the Songhay Empire, which of the functional aspects of empire were the most important? Was this because of the unique circumstances of the Songhay Empire or is it a general characteristic of empires?

- How Empires rise?
    1. Do any reasons for the rise of empires seem especially important? What is it about those reasons that gives them more weight?
    2. What factors propelled Japan toward the formation of an empire in the 19th century? Were there any events or historical realities crucial to this process?
- How Empires fall?
    1. Once an empire begins to decline, can anything be done to stop it? Why or why not?
    2. Of all the factors that contribute to the decline of an empire, which are the most important?
    3. The Ottoman Empire existed for a very long time, and its decline was a very complex process of many factors that changed over time. In what particular areas did Ottomans seem to be the weakest?
- Perspective
    1. What is the relationship between empire and nation as forms of political organization? Can they exist at the same time in any one state? How does one influence the other?
    2. How might the average citizen of the United States around the year 1900 have experienced the ideas of empire and nation?
    3. How did the rise of mass culture and politics change empires at the end of the 19th century?

MODULE LEVEL QUESTIONS

- What is a "sphere of influence" and how does this concept relate to the geographic distribution and identity of a given empire?
- What was the Meiji Restoration and how did it affect the foundation of the Japanese Empire in East Asia during the late 19th century?
- "Empires are founded primarily upon clear, strategic geopolitical goals." Respond to this statement (and be sure in the process to address the various factors involved in the rise of empires).
- What factors explain the long decline of the Ottoman Empire? Is it fair to say that the entire period of the 17th through the 20th century was one of stagnation and decline for this polity, or was it more complex?
- How did the rise of mass culture and politics transform the condition of empire at the end of the 19th century?

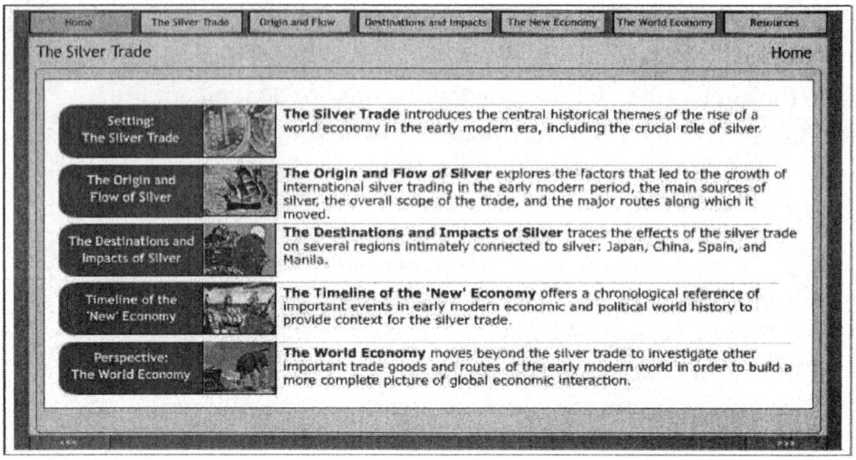

THE SILVER TRADE AND THE WORLD ECONOMY (1500-1700)

This module encourages the student to investigate the patterns of the Early Modern world economy by focusing on how the silver trade served as a vital link, bringing regional economies closer together and ensuring lasting effects.

SECTION QUESTIONS

- Destinations and Impacts
    1. What effects did the silver trade have on early modern Japan?
    2. What role did the Fuggers and other European bankers play in the European silver trade?
    3. What role did the silver trade play in the economic downturns of the mid-17th century?
    4. How did the silver trade affect early modern Spain?
    5. What role did European states play in the early modern silver trade?

Module Level Questions

- Why was trade in silver so important in the early modern world economy? Be sure in your answer to address China's role in this historical dynamic.
- Where were the major sources of silver during the "Silver Century"? Which states benefited from control over these areas and in what ways?
- What role did the Fugger family and other banking houses play in the European silver trade?
- "The silver trade was as much a curse as it was a blessing for the Spanish." Discuss this statement, asserting whether or not you believe it to be more or less accurate, justifying your argument with examples from the module.
- What was the mita and how did it figure into the silver trade?

EXPLORING A RENAISSANCE PAINTING

This interactive module is designed to offer students a dynamic, enriching learning experience. The centerpiece module, Raphael's *School of Athens*, is brought to life using innovative pedagogy and today's technology, allowing students to click on figures in the painting to learn about their significance in history. The module also explains the content in which Raphael's *School of Athens* was painted and illustrates how religion, philosophy, and music influence Renaissance art.

EXERCISE

1. Create your own *School of Athens*. Before you begin, you might consider the following: who or what to include (and exclude); what form and materials to use; where the final creation might be displayed; who will have access to your creation; whether you want to install your creation permanently or alter it over time; whether your creation will be a public or private expression (or perhaps both); what people, ideas, and mediums influence your decisions; and what your creation may reveal about you.

2. Choose a present-day artifact that best provides a commentary on our time the way Raphael's painting does on the *Renaissance* and explain your selection.
3. Who or what is omitted from the *School of Athens*? What is the significance of these absences?
4. Click here to consider issues of the painting's formal construction.
5. After studying the *School of Athens* and the *Stanza della Segnatura*, design a library. How would you collect and organize the books? What interests would guide you? Which personifications would best represent the elements of the library, and why? Who would have access to the library?
6. Throughout **Exploring a Renaissance Painting** we have been emphasizing harmony between philosophical traditions and in terms of composition, figure, and expression. Yet Raphael includes elements of opposition and conflict. Discuss the ways in which Raphael both represents and restrains the forces of discord. For instance, how might his efforts have related to those of his patrons, Pope Julius II and Leo X?
7. Having read briefly about some of the philosophers depicted in the *School of Athens*, place three or four of them in a "teacher-disciple" order. Remember that sometimes a disciple depicted in the painting is not the *physical* pupil of a great teacher, but rather learned about him from writings or word-of-mouth long after the "teacher" died. How are these relationships explored through composition and other elements in the painting?
8. Create a dialogue between the painting's central figures – Plato and Aristotle – based on what you now know about Platonic and Aristotelian thought. Have each of the two philosophers mention at least two other figures in the painting so that their relationships to those figures are revealed?
9. In the *School of Athens*, many of the figures are paired with particular objects. How do these objects speak to the ideas and character of the figures with which they are paired? What other objects might you associate with the figures depicted in the *School of Athens*?

10. Gesture and body language play central roles in the *School of Athens*. Discuss two or three gestures or poses in the painting in terms of their significance to the figures depicted as well as to the viewer's response to the work as a whole.
11. Much of the power of the *School of Athens* derives from Raphael's deliberate, exacting, and exquisite use of architecture and perspective construction in the design and conception of the fresco. In what ways would our reading of this painting change if the figures depicted in the *School of Athens* were placed in a different setting?

WARFARE IN EARLY MODERN EUROPE: 1494 - 1648

This module investigates the nature of warfare in early modern Europe. By exploring the changing nature of military technology and tactics, as well as illustrating the historical context of important wars from this period, the module presents the student with a solid introduction to both the military history of the time and the ways that the changing methods of warfare transformed politics and economics.

READINGS:

- The Battle of Breitenfeld (1631)
- The Adventurous Simplicissimus (1669)
- The Destruction of Magdeburg (1631)
- De Jure Belli ac Pacis [On the Law of War and Peace] (1625), Hugo Grotius
- Treaty of Westphalia, October 24, 1648, Münster, Germany

- Revolution
  1. What was the military revolution?
  2. What advantage did the so-called Gunpowder Empires hold over other powers in the early modern period?
  3. How did the formation of large, standing armies help influence the centralization of state authority during this period?
  4. How would the average fortification built in 1700 differ from one built in 1400?

5. What social transformations came about in the wake of the military revolution?

MODULE LEVEL QUESTIONS

- What is the significance of the phrase cuius regio, eius religio?
- What was the so-called military revolution?
- What advantage did the so-called Gunpowder Empires hold over other powers at this time?
- Did improvements in military technology have anything to do with the English victory over the Spanish Armada? If so, what were they?
- What was the significance of the development of more flexible military units on Western battlefields during the early modern period?

GOD, GOLD AND GLORY: COLUMBUS AND THE AGE OF EXPLORATION, 1413 - 1776

This module explores the period 1415-1776, in which European exploration of the world began in earnest. The module covers Europe's initial overseas forays, the beginnings of commercial and military expansionism, and the historical implications of expansion both for Europe and the wider world. Employing interactive maps, images, documents, and exercises, the module reviews this history from multiple perspectives, charting the intersections of the technological, the economic, the cultural, and the religious factors that both led to and ultimately shaped European exploration and expansion at this time.

READINGS:

- An Aztec Account (1528)
- James Barbot, A Voyage to the New Calabar River (1699)
- Description of a Voyage from Lisbon to the Island of São Thomè (c. 1540), Anonymous Portuguese Pilot
- The Memoirs of the Conquistador Bernal Díaz del Castillo, excerpts
- Bartolomé de Las Casas, In Defense of the Indians (1550)
- The Bull Inter Caetera (Alexander VI), May 4, 1493
- The Bull Romanus Pontifex (Nicholas V), January 8, 1455
- Juan Ginés de Sepúlveda, Democrates Secundus, or The Just Causes of War Against the Indians (1547)
- Fra Soncino: Letter to Ludovico Sforza (1497)

- The Requirement (1526)
- Treaty between Spain and Portugal concluded at Tordesillas; June 7, 1494 Ratified by Spain, July 2, 1494; Ratified by Portugal, September 5, 1494.
- Columbus's Letter to Gabriel Sanchez (1493)
- The Journal of Christopher Columbus, translated by Clements R. Markham

SECTION QUESTIONS

- Pre-Columbian Exploration
    1. What significance lay in the Portuguese conquest of Ceuta in 1415?
    2. What international circumstances helped encouraged European exploration of the Atlantic in the 14th and 15th centuries?
    3. What differences were there between the patterns of exploration undertaken from northern and southern Europe?
    4. What did "discovery" mean in the context of European exploration? What sorts of things were discovered?
    5. What was the *volto do mar largo* and why was it important in the history of Atlantic exploration?
- 1492
    1. It's often been said that Europe's periods of expansion can be summed up with the phrase "for God, gold, and glory." How accurate do you think this statement is when applied to the period 1415-1776?
    2. What reasons helped make Columbus and his voyage so well known in the annals of western exploration?
    3. What was the Columbian Exchange?
- Perspectives (Thought Questions)
    1. What was the "plantation system" and how did encourage exploration?
    2. How did the age of exploration incorporate Europe in a truly world economy?

Module Level Questions

- What was the Columbian Exchange?
- What was the volta do mar largo and why was it significant in the history of western exploration?
- Comment on this statement: "The travels of men like Marco Polo and Niccoló Conti substantially encouraged European exploration of the world in 15th-16th centuries."
- How did the Atlantic System tie Europe, Africa, and the Americas together?

THE FRENCH REVOLUTION: THE SUMMER OF 1789 AND THE ORIGINS OF THE FRENCH REVOLUTION

This module examines the conditions in France that helped precipitate revolution in the late 1780s. It also reviews the major events during the first year of the French Revolution, providing a sound introduction to this vital period of modern history.

READINGS:

- Cahiers de doléances from 1789, Edited and translated by Merrick Whitcombe
- Decrees of the National Assembly, August 10-11, 1789
- Dispatches from Paris (April-July 1789), From Estates General to National Assembly
- Motion of the Herring Women of La Halle
- Letter from the Mayor of Dunkirk to the Intendant of Flanders, July 25, 1789
- October Days Depositions
- Recollections (1813), Guy-Marie Sallier
- Declaration of the Rights of Man and Citizen, Approved by the National Assembly of France, August 26, 1789
- What is the Third Estate? (Qu'est-ce que le tiers état?), Emmanuel, Joseph Sieyes
- The King's Closing Speech, June 23, 1789
- Tennis Court Oath, June 20, 1789
- The Declaration of Independence (1776), The Unanimous Declaration of the Thirteen United States of America

- Declaration of the Rights of Women, 1791, Olympe de Gouge

SECTION QUESTIONS

- Settings
    1. What do you think Alfred Cobban meant when he called revolution the "strategic center" of modern history? Do you agree or disagree with him?
    2. What are the typical stages that a revolution undergoes?
    3. What does it mean that pre-revolutionary French society was "corporate" in nature?
    4. How might the various factors that contributed to the French Revolution have encouraged each other?
    5. In what ways do you think the American Revolution affected the French Revolution?
- A Fateful Year
    1. Why was the original voting system of the Estates General disadvantageous to the Third Estate?
    2. Why were the events of the October Days so significant, both to the history of the French Revolution, and to the role of women in revolution in general?
    3. What was the Great Fear and what circumstances caused it?

MODULE LEVEL QUESTIONS

- What does it mean that pre-1789 France was a "society of orders"? What were they?
- Why did the Great Fear develop in the summer of 1789?
- What was the Tennis Court Oath?
- "Jean-Jacques Rousseau, Voltaire, and other Enlightenment figures caused the French Revolution." Comment: is this statement true or false?
- What was the significance of the "October Days" of 1789?

THE ORDER OF THE DAY - TERROR IN THE FRENCH REVOLUTION, 1792 - 1794

This module explores the development of the Terror in the French Revolution. It illustrates the various phases of the Terror, from the urban violence of the summer of 1792 through the backlash in the wake of Thermidor in 1794, and reviews the factors behind the radicalization of the Revolution and the genesis of the Terror.

READINGS:

- Act passed by the Convention on 27 Brumaire an II, (November 17, 1793)
- The Constitution of 1793
- Extract from the Register of Deliberations of the General Council of the Commune of Paris, (September 11, 1793)
- Decree Regulating Divorce (September 20, 1792)
- The Indictment of Louis XVI (December 11, 1792)
- Decree Establishing the Levée en Masse (August 23, 1793)
- Proceedings of the National Convention (September 5, 1793)
- The Law of 22 Prairial, June 10, 1794 (22 Prairial, Year 11)
- Report on the Principles of Political Morality, (February 5, 1794), Maximilien Robespierre
- The Social Contract (1762), Jean-Jacques Rousseau
- Report to the Convention on Behalf of the Committee of Public Safety, (October 10, 1793), Louis de Saint-Just
- An Answer to the Impertinent Question: But What is a Sans-Culotte? April 1793

- The Law of Suspects, (September 17, 1793)
- Decree Establishing the Worship of the Supreme Being, (May 7, 1794)

SECTION QUESTIONS

- Settings
    1. Can the Terror be compared to the Great Fear of 1789? Why or why not?
    2. In which phase of the French Revolution did the Terror occur?
- Radicalization
    1. Why did the king and his family try to flee France in the summer of 1791?
    2. What factors help explain why the mood of France changed toward the end of the summer of 1792?
    3. Looking at the various factors that helped radicalize the Revolution in 1791 and 1792, which do you think was most important, and why?
    4. What effect did the Declaration of Pillnitz have upon the Revolution?
    5. What role did popular print play in the radicalization of the Revolution?
- Terror
    1. In what ways did the Terror of June-July 1794 differ from that of summer 1793 to January 1794?
    2. What role did the sans-culottes play in the Terror?
    3. Why did economic measures (such as the Maximum) assume such importance for some groups during the radical phase of the French Revolution?
- Conclusion
    1. What are the basic schools of thought on the historical interpretation of the Terror?
    2. About what do the differing historical interpretations of the Terror seem to disagree? What ideas do they share?
    3. What cultural or social legacies do you think the Terror might have left in France?

MODULE LEVEL QUESTIONS

- What was the Terror?
- What factors radicalized France in 1791-1792, pushing the country down a path to Terror?
- Comment on the factional strife within the National Convention in 1792-1793.
- What function did the pressure of the sans-culottes serve in escalating the Terror?
- Describe one way in which the government in Paris during the Terror sought to remake the fabric of French culture and society?
- Referring to the violent extremes of the Terror, one print from 1794 commented, "It is dreadful, but necessary." Do you agree?

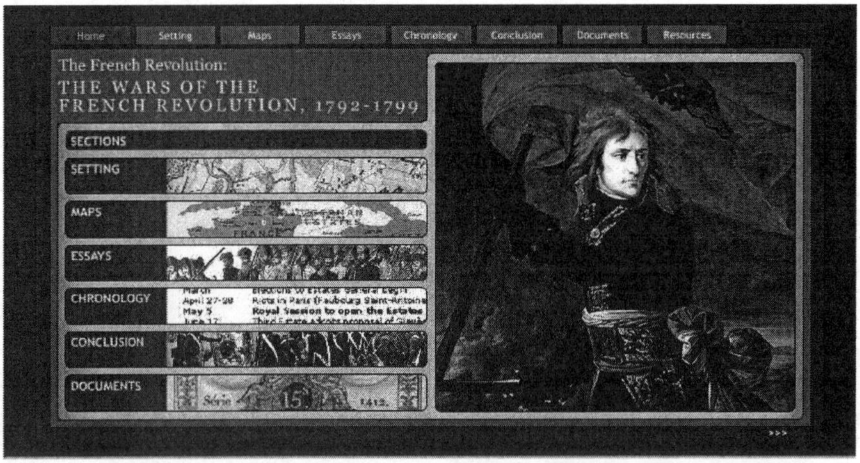

THE WARS OF THE FRENCH REVOLUTION, 1792 - 1799

This module explores the fabric of the wars of the French Revolution in two ways. First, it presents a series of four interactive maps detailing the military campaigns from 1792 to 1799, covering the rise and fall of the First Coalition, the beginning of the Second Coalition, and Napoleon's ill-fated invasion of Egypt. Second, it provides a series of essays on topics related to the conduct of the war. As a whole, the module offers an introductory survey of the contours of revolutionary warfare in Europe, from the rise of the Revolution through its ultimate demise at the hands of Napoleon.

READINGS:

- Charitas [On the Civil Oath in France], April 13, 1791, Pope Pius VI
- Statement of French Foreign Policy, April 14, 1792
- French Declaration of War on Austria, April 20, 1792
- The Brunswick Manifesto, July 25, 1792
- French Declaration of War against Britain and the Netherlands, February 1, 1793
- Decree of National Convention for National Conscription, (February 1, 1793)
- Treaty of Basle, April 5, 1795
- Proclamation to the Army of Italy, March 27, 1796, Napoleon Bonaparte
- Treaty of Campio Formio, October 17, 1797
- Treaty between France and the Cisalpine Republic, February 21, 1798

SECTION QUESTIONS

- Settings
    1. Why did certain groups within the French revolutionary government favor a war?
    2. To what extent did France's early opponents oppose the mission of the Revolution, and to what degree did their actions indicate more practical, strategic concerns?
- Essays
    1. In what ways were the French armies of the revolutionary period dramatically new and different in European history? How might these factors have made a difference in the life of an average soldier at the time?
    2. Why do you think the local leaders who helped set up the "sister republics" across Europe consented to what no doubt seemed like the creation of nothing more than another French satellite?
    3. What elements of Old Regime international relations persisted into the period of the revolutionary wars?
    4. What were the important moments in the rise of Napoleon Bonaparte to power in France?

MODULE LEVEL QUESTIONS

- What forces within France pushed the country toward war in 1792?
- How did "sister republics" like the Batavian Republic come into being in the 1790s?
- In what ways were the armies of revolutionary France new, and in what ways was this an asset to France?
- To what degree were the war aims of France's early opponents Austria and Prussia centered on the Revolution itself?
- What major events elevated Napoleon to a high military command by 1796?

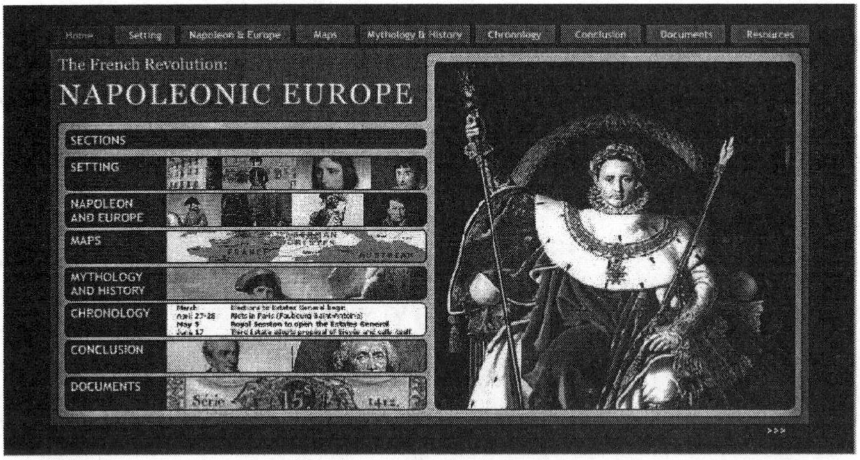

NAPOLEONIC EUROPE

This module examines the character and implications of the regime of Napoleon Bonaparte upon both France and Europe. Incorporating investigations of the military and administrative facets of Napoleon's career and legacy, the module reviews for the student Napoleon's rise to power, his actions while in control of France, and his lasting efforts to restructure the very fabric of Europe's political and social identity.

READINGS:

- Constitution of the Year VIII, December 13, 1799
- Napoleon's Presentation of the Constitution of the Year VIII to the French People, December 15, 1799
- Concordat with the Papacy; signed, September 10, 1801, published in Paris, Easter Sunday, April 8, 1802.
- The French Civil Code, the Code Napoléon, March 1803 - March 1804. Preliminary Title Of the Publication, Effect, and Application of the Laws in General Article 1)
- Imperial Catechism, April 4, 1806
- Napoleon Bonaparte, The Berlin Decree (1806)
- Treaties of Tilsit; July 7-9, 1807
- Prussian Edict of Emancipation (1807)
- Addresses to the German Nation (1808), Johann Gottlieb Fichte
- Napoleon's letter to Tsar Alexander 1, explaining the French Invasion of Russia; July 1, 1812.
- The Memoirs of Sergeant Bourgogne: 1812-1813 (Excerpt)
- Constitutional Charter of 1814, June 4, 1814

- First Treaty of Paris, May 30, 1814
- Napoleon's Proclamation to the French on his Return from Elba, March 1, 1815
- Considerations on the Principal Events of the French Revolution (1818), Madame de Staël

SECTION QUESTIONS

- Napoleon and Europe
    1. Why was the enormity of the Grande Armée of 1812 actually a detriment to success for the French in the Russian campaign?
    2. What factors about the Peninsular campaign made it particularly dangerous for the Napoleonic regime?
    3. Which of Napoleon's reforms persisted after the downfall of his regime? Why do you think these remained in place while others did not?
    4. How did Napoleon's administrative reforms help him establish tighter, more personal control over France?
    5. How did Napoleon reach out and garner support from the various segments of French society?
- Conclusion
    1. What do you think about the relationship between Napoleon and the French Revolution? Was he the culmination of the Revolution's goals, or their ultimate destruction?
    2. What were the major goals the delegates wrestled with at the Congress of Vienna?

MODULE LEVEL QUESTIONS

- Do you think Napoleon Bonaparte qualifies as the heir of the French Revolution or as its executioner?
- How did Napoleon's administrative reforms help him establish tighter, more personal control over France?
- What were the principal elements behind the downfall of Napoleon's empire in 1814?
- How effective was Napoleon's "Continental System" in weakening Britain, and how did this policy effect France and the rest of Europe?
- How did the delegates to the Congress of Vienna resolve the major issues they faced at the dawn of a post-Napoleonic Europe?

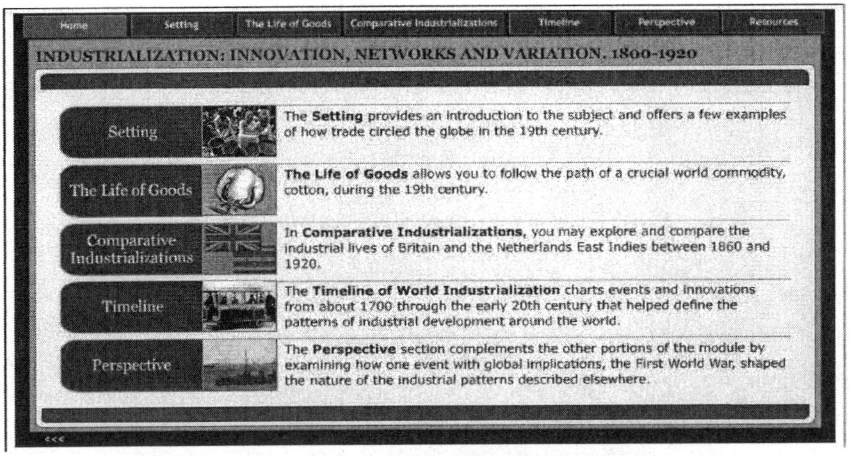

INDUSTRIALIZATION IN WORLD HISTORY

This module explores the historical process of industrialization on a global scale, discerns patterns of development that helped drive this process, locates representative interregional patterns of commerce, identifies illustrative transformations of technology and organization, and explains the role of industrialization in shaping 20th-century society.

READINGS:

- Social Life, Mary Bateson
- The Cotton Trade (1857), J. Baynes
- Surabaya: the Sugar Centre (1923), Frank G. Carpenter
- On the Coffee Estates (1923), Frank G. Carpenter
- Across Java by Rail (1923), Frank G. Carpenter
- Address on the Factory Act (1832), Michael Sadler
- A Railroad Mint — What the Legend Says (1868), Samuel Clemens (Mark Twain)
- Organization of a Rubber, Coffee, and Sisal Estate in East Java (1923), John A. Fowler
- National and General Importance of the Cotton Manufacture (1823), Richard Guest
- The Steam Loom (1823), Richard Guest
- Survey of the economic conditions of the indigenous people of Java and Madura, 1921, W. Huender
- The Submarine Telegraph Between Dover and Calais, *The London Journal*, Sept. 28, 1850
- A Guide to Bombay (1889), James Mackenzie Maclean

- The Influence of Sea Power on History: 1660-1783 (1896), A.T. Mahan
- The Cotton Exchange of New Orleans, Report of the Industrial Commission, 1901
- Sir Charles W. Macara, Bart. (1917), A Study of Modern Lancashire, Victorian Manchester
- Max Havelaar, Or the Coffee Auctions of the Dutch Trading Company (1860), Multatuli (E.D. Dekker)
- Twelve Years a Slave (1853), Solomon Northup
- The World's Great Assembly (1851), English Monthly Tract Society, London: J F Shaw
- A Visit to India, China, and Japan In the Year 1853, Bayard Taylor (canals)
- A Visit to India, China, and Japan In the Year 1853, Bayard Taylor (manufacturing)
- The Principles of Scientific Management, Frederick Winslow Taylor
- Cotton, The Plant, Growth, and Distribution, Perry Walton
- Problems of Modern Industry (1902), Sidney and Beatrice Webb
- The Memoirs of Count Witte, Sergei Witte
- International Organizations in the 20th Century, Amnesty International's Appeals for Action, 2001
- 15-Point Program for Implementing Human Rights in International Peace-keeping Operations, Amnesty International
- Human Rights Violations Worldwide Detailed in Amnesty International's Annual Report 2001
- Object and Mandate, 1999, Amnesty International
- A Biography of Henry Dunant (1828-1910)
- *A Memory of Solferino*, excerpts, Henry Dunant
- The Emblem and the Flag of 1914, from *Olympism, Selected Writings,* Pierre de Coubertin
- The Covenant of the League of Nations
- League of Nations Membership
- The Fundamental Principles of the Olympic Charter
- Sites of the Olympic Games
- Red Cross Main Relief Operations, 1919-2000
- Restoration of the Olympic Games, from "Physical Exercises in the Modern World", Pierre de Coubertin
- Fiftieth Anniversary of the Universal Declaration of Human Rights, United Nations

- Growth in United Nations Membership, 1945-2000
- Preamble to the Charter of the United Nations
- Vienna Proclamation, The International Committee of the Red Cross
- League of Nations Speech, September 25, 1919, excerpts, Woodrow Wilson
- World Bank Mission Statement
- 10 Things You Never Knew About the World Bank

SECTION QUESTIONS

- The life of goods
    1. Having seen how labor was used to harvest the vast cotton fields of the American South, what form of labor was most crucial to the cotton economy of the United States?
        a. Agricultural labor (e.g. slaves, sharecroppers)
        b. River pilots
        c. Low-paying factory labor
        d. Female factory workers
    2. What effects did the advent and expansion of steam-powered travel have on the flow of cotton and, by extension, the flow of world trade?
        a. Steam enhanced the speed, dependability, and range of transport while reducing the cost of freight, thus making it possible to cheaply move such goods as cotton from one continent to another.
        b. Steam had little impact on trade, the patterns of which had largely been well-established centuries before steam's arrival on the world stage.
        c. The use of steam was severely limited because of the problems involved in fueling steam vessels, so much so that its impact on world trade was negligible.
        d. Though steam enhanced the speed of ocean transport, the amount of cargo space given over to fuel supply prevented this method of shipping from being profitable.

3. What role did the market demand for cotton play in the development of British industrialization?
    a. Little role at all, since governmental incentives spurred the growth of industry more than any other factor.
    b. Somewhat, though the primary factor driving industrial growth in Britain was competition with the United States.
    c. It played a substantial role, because the rising demand of British consumers (as well as consumers overseas) drove manufacturers to produce more cotton goods.
    d. Only a small role, because the New England factories began dominating the world market for cotton goods as early as the 1850s, shutting out British exports.
4. What role did Indian cotton garments play in the world cotton market?
    a. Only a small role, given the dominance of British and American manufactured garments after the 1820s.
    b. A major role, because of the market dominance they enjoyed in much of the world and because their reputation for quality inspired British manufacturers to "out-produce" them.
    c. The dominant role, largely due to the massive export of cotton garments to China and Japan.
    d. Not much of a role at all, once the American cotton industry expanded early in the 19th century.

5. How important were the ports of Japan to its process of industrialization?
    a. Not very important at all because Japanese industrialization was largely a land-locked phenomenon.
    b. Extremely important, given the expanded role that Japanese seaborne commerce played in the world economy in the late 19th and early 20th centuries.
    c. Not important at all, because Japan was largely self-sufficient in the raw materials and power sources necessary for heavy industrial growth.
    d. Very important, because Japan's export of machinery proved to be the primary factor in its industrial development during the late 19th century.

MODULE LEVEL QUESTIONS

- Explain briefly some of the general ways (at least 3) that the process of industrialization has changed the lives of people over the past five hundred years.
- What were some of the important indications that the world's economy was growing more interconnected from 1500 on?
- How does the device of the commodity chain help explain the world historical connections so crucial to the processes of industrialization?
- Agree or disagree with the following statement: "World War One had a tremendous effect on the global economy." Be sure to refer to examples from the module in your answer.
- How did labor practices change in both Britain and the Netherlands East Indies as a result of industrialization?

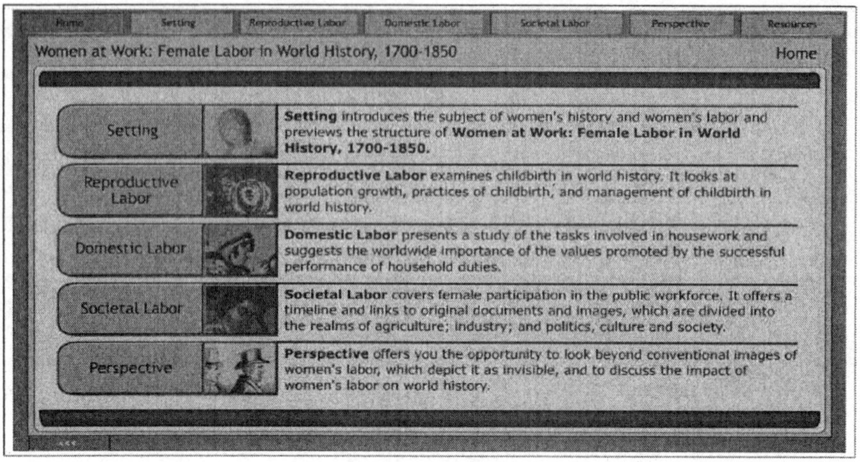

WOMEN AT WORK: FEMALE LABOR IN WORLD HISTORY (1700-1850)

This module examines the various productive roles played by women around the world during the 18th and early 19th centuries. Consideration of women's reproductive, domestic, and societal contributions and of regional variations and changes over the era enables students to come to a deeper understanding of the role of gender in world history.

READINGS:

- *The Skilful Housewife's Book*, 1846 (excerpts), Mrs. L. G. Abell
- *Housekeeping Book of Susanna Whatman* (excerpts)
- *American Woman's Home*, 1869 (excerpts), Catharine Beecher and Harriet Beecher Stowe
- *The Book of Household Management*, 1864 (excerpts), Isabella Beeton
- *The American Frugal Housewife*, 1854 (excerpts), Mrs. Child
- *The Gentlewoman*, 1864 (excerpt), Anonymous
- Reading: Proper care of Teeth and Hair

- The Beauty of a Home Garden
- Keeping the Entrance Clean
- Fostering a Gentle Environment for Children
- Maintaining the Bedchamber Fires
- On the Storing of Food
- How to Make a Bed
- Care of the Cellar
- Table Manners for Children
- The Value of Bathing
- How to Wash Dishes
- A Warning about Indulgence
- Parlor Upkeep
- The Value of Early Rising
- List of Items in Season
- Moth-Proofing One's Clothing
- Winter Care for the Water Pump
- How to Make Soap
- How to Soften Water
- Some Common Methods for Making Dye
- That Essential Tool, the Cork
- The Value of Reading
- How to Preserve Eggs
- Setting the Breakfast Table
- The Teething Child
- The Usefulness of a Home Garden
- How to Clean Curtains and Upholstery
- How to Make Candles
- Caring for Marble Steps
- How to Catch Rats and Mice
- Setting the Dinner Table
- Sample Menus for Dinner Parties
- The Importance of Breakfast
- A Warning about Well Water
- Washing, Starching, and Ironing
- Economizing in the Kitchen
- How to Cook Pigeons
- The Value of Doing Needlework
- How to Bake a Loaf Cake
- Opposition to Female Labor, Abbas Pasha
- Petition of Parisian Women to King Louis XVI, 1789 (excerpts)

- *General View of the coal Trade of Scotland*, 1812 (excerpts), R. Bald
- Letter from Savannah, Sunday 7th March 1858, Barbara Bodichon
- Diary Excerpt of Helen Carpenter
- Letter of Women Workers in Paris appealing to the government (1848)
- Courtauld Silk Mill Workforce, 1825
- Some Considerations upon Street-Walkers with A Proposal for lessening the present Number of them, [1726], Daniel Defoe
- Declaration of the Rights of Women, 1791, Olympe de Gouge
- Journal Entry, Fanny Calderon de la Barca
- Personal Testimony, Sor Juana Ines de la Cruz
- *The Fable of the Bees: Or, Private Vices, Public Benefits*, 1724, De Mandeville, Bernard.
- *An Account of the Rise, Progress, and Present State of the Magdalen Hospital, for the reception of Penitent Prostitutes*, 1770 (excerpts), Dr. Dodd
- Testimony of a Dressmaker, Feb. 11, 1841
- *The State of the Poor,* 1797 (excerpt), Eden, Sir Frederic Morton
- Testimony before the Children's Employment Commission of the British Parliament (1842)
- The Lowell Factory Girl
- Excerpt from Robert Fortune's Travel Journal
- *Gentleman's Magazine* (July, 1801)
- Last requests of Juana Guancaparoba, 1767.
- A Cuban Planter's View of Female Slaves, G. M. Hall
- Prices of Male and Female Slaves
- New Voyage to the Isles of America, Jean-Baptiste Labat
- *Journal of a West India Proprietor* (Excerpt), M.G. Lewis
- *A Voyage to the Coast of Africa in 1758*(Excerpt), John Lindsay
- Letter of Philadelphia Seamstresses, July 1862
- "A Week in the Mill" *Lowell Offering*, October 1845
- History of the Slave Insurrection in the North of Saint-Domingue, Antoine Métral
- Personal Letter (Excerpt), Lady Mary Wortley Montagu
- *The Ladies' Dictionary*, excerpt, 1694

- Women on the Trail to Oregon, Oregon Provisional Emigration Society
- *A Mother's Advice to Her Absent Daughters*, 1822, Lady Pennington
- "My spinning wheel is dear to me, my sister", Ratanbai
- *Emile, or On Education*, Book V (excerpts), Jean-Jacques Rousseau
- Whisper to a Bride, 1850 *(excerpt)*, Mrs. L.H. Sigourney
- Letter to English Workers, Flora Tristan
- "Ain't I A Woman", 1851, Sojourner Truth (Account by Frances Gage, 1881)
- *Reflections on the Present Condition of the Female Sex; with Suggestions for its Improvement,* 1798 (excerpts), Priscilla Wakefield
- Talk of the President of the United States to the Beloved Men of the Cherokee Nation, August 29, 1796, George Washington
- "A Vindication of the Rights of Woman," 1792 (excerpts), Mary Wollstonecraft
- *Inquire within for Anything you want to know*, 1858 (excerpts), Anonymous
- *The House Book: Or, A Manual of Domestic Economy*, 1840 (excerpts), Miss Leslie
- *First Principles of Household Management*, 1879 (excerpts), Maria Parloa
- *How to Live: Saving and Wasting, Or, Domestic Economy Illustrated*, 1860 (excerpt), Solon Robinson
- *A New System of Domestic Cookery: Formed upon Principles of Economy, and Adapted to the Use of Private Families*, 1807 (excerpt) M.E.K. Rundell
- The *Ladies' Self Instructor in Millinery* (excerpt), Anonymous
- *American Cookery*, 1796 (excerpt), Amelia Simmons

SECTION QUESTIONS

- **Reproductive Labor**
    1. As presented in "Reproductive Labor through History," several factors affect birth rates, including the different ideas societies have about appropriate household size. During this era in Africa, for example, large families were prized, whereas in Japan, small households were considered ideal. How do you think birth rate and household size might have affected attitudes towards motherhood? Do you suppose motherhood would have been more or less prized in societies with higher birth rates? Give examples to support your answer.
    2. On the basis of customs discussed in "Practices of Reproductive Labor," what strikes you more: the diversity of the childbearing experience across the world or the commonality of it? Give examples to support your answer.
    3. In the examples in "Management of Reproductive Labor," different groups of people attempted to make decisions about childbearing among local populations. Who do you think is in the best position to make decisions about reproduction? What should the role be for people implicated in the decision-making – for example, community leaders, religions leaders, slaveholders, and fathers?
    4. What does the study of reproductive labor tell us about gender roles during this period of history? To what extent were these roles shared in different areas of the world? How have attitudes towards gender changed over time? Can you draw any comparisons between what you've learned here and what you know about reproductive labor today?

- **Domestic Labor**

  1. House plans around the world circa 1750.

  a. Courtyard House in Northern China

  1. In the past, the ideal Chinese household contained several generations under one roof. How do you think a woman's responsibilities within the home changed depending on the presence of her grown sons, their wives, and their children? Do you think her job was made easier or harder? Why?
  2. In contrast to Western houses, the uses of most of the rooms in a Chinese house were flexible depending on the needs of the family. There was no permanent dining room, for example; rather, tables were set up for mealtimes. How do you think a flexible attitude to space impacted on women's labor within the home?
  3. How would you characterize the differences between public and private space within the Chinese home, and what was the significance of each? Was there at the time, and is there now, an equivalent distinction made in the West? How might this distinction impact women and their labor in the home?

  b. *Yurt* in Mongolia

  1. *Yurts* were (and still are) common among various nomadic people across parts of Mongolia, Afghanistan, and the former Soviet Union. Why do you think this form of housing has been so popular?

2. The space inside a *yurt* was small by Western standards, and household items all had assigned positions: certain chests stored rugs, clothing, and utensils, and certain vessels held various food items and milk. How would typical household tasks – such as washing clothes and utensils or preparing meals – have been affected by this type of space and its organization? Do you think domestic labor would have been less or more difficult in such surroundings?
3. The use of space inside a *yurt* was organized by gender, with separate quadrants devoted to men and to women and children. What do you think the effects of such organization would have been on relations between the sexes? Can you think of effects on women and the tasks they performed in that space?

c. Tent in Northeastern Sudan
   1. For the Mahria people of northeastern Sudan, tent dwelling suited a nomadic lifestyle in which people migrated according to the needs of their animal herds – traveling northwards in search of good pastures in the rainy season and returning south in the dry season to be close to permanent wells. (Such tent dwellings are still used today.) How do you think the division of labor evolved so that women were responsible for the construction of the tent? What do you think men and other family members did while women constructed tents?

2. Mahrian women always constructed their tents lengthwise from north to south with the front entrance on the northwest corner. Why do you think they used this particular orientation? How might their various domestic tasks have been influenced by the daily rotation of the sun? Can you think of similar examples from other cultures of the ways in which the sun or weather could affect the performance of daily domestic labor?
3. Mahrian women were also responsible for milking the camels; they used the milk to make tea and churned butter. But the men and boys were often away from camp, sometimes for weeks at a time, herding the camels while the women, children, and old people stayed behind. From a woman's point of view, what would be the advantages of those times when the men, boys, and camels were absent? What would be the disadvantages? How would women's routines change depending on the movement of the herds?

2. Household Tasks and Their Values

While individual housekeeping tasks all have immediate goals – such as elimination of dirt or the satisfaction of hunger – they also contribute to broader, less direct and less immediate goals for the successful functioning of the home and society. For each of the following tasks of the colonial housewife, listed in Group A, choose one or more goals from Group B that you think are met by the successful performance of the task. State how many of the goals are personal and how many add to the household. How many overlap?

Group A: Tasks

Attending a tea party	Cooking	House cleaning
Shopping for household goods		Churchgoing
Doing laundry	Letter writing	Soap making
Clothes mending	Embroidering	Personal grooming
Stocking the linen closet		
Clothes ironing	Food shopping	Reading a book
Training servants	Clothes sewing	Gardening
Reading a newspaper	Visiting friends or neighbors	
Conserving food	Seasonal cleaning	
Watching at a sickbed	Hosting a tea party	

Group B: Goals

House upkeep	Ties to local community
Hygiene	Ties to homeland
Marital relations	
Prestige	
Self-Improvement	
Thrift	

3. Domestic Labor and Cultural Difference

As a newly arrived English colonist in North America, a colonial housewife inhabited an unfamiliar world, although it might not have been entirely alien to her. How do you think some of the tasks and goals listed above differed in other colonial settings during the same era, where the potential clash between cultures might have been more severe?

For example you can consider how experiences would have differed for an African slave in the Caribbean, a British housewife in India, a Spanish housewife in Latin America, a Chinese housewife in Southeast Asia, a Dutch housewife in the East Indies, or other cross-cultural examples of which you may be aware. Would the concerns of these women be the same? Would the challenges be greater? Can you think of additional domestic tasks that would be dictated by such different environments?

MODULE LEVEL QUESTIONS

- What features do the disciplines of women's history and world history share? What is to be gained from combining these two perspectives on the past?
- Explain the differences between the 3 main forms of women's work described in the module.
- What factors during the period 1700-1850 contributed to the changing gender roles of domestic labor?
- What does the concept of "separate spheres" entail? How has this affected women's working lives, both at home and in society?
- Did practices of reproductive labor change substantially from 1700 to 1850? If so, in what ways?

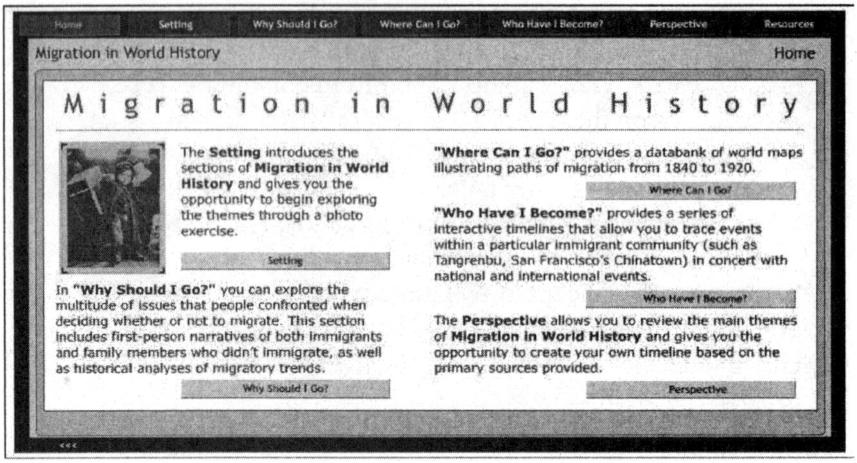

WORLD MIGRATION (1840-1920)

This module encourages students to explore two rarely emphasized connections in the study of migration - the scale and direction of Asian and European migrations and the experiences of long-distance immigrants and the resulting effects on the families and community members that were left behind.

READINGS:

- What Does North America Offer to the German Emigrant? (1853), Gottfried Menzel
- Experiences of an Investigator in the Steerage, Excerpts from reports of the U.S. Immigration Commission, 1911
- The Wife of Paul Benjamin, (*Difficulties with the "Near East" Quota)*
- From Plotzk to Boston, Mary Antin
- One Family, Two Worlds: an Italian Family's Correspondence across the Atlantic, 1901–1922, (excerpts)
- Life Stories of Two Chinese Emigrants to Hawaii, Clarence E. Glick
- The Board of Foreign Missions of the Presbyterian Church Annual Reports (Excerpts), 1891
- Poems of Chinese Immigrants to America
- Description of Coolie Labor Processing (1912), J.R.O. Aldworth, Controller of Labour, Malay
- Account of Immigration, Charles Smirnoff
- Two Accounts of Norwegian Emigration to Hawaii

- Review of German Emigration, 1881
- The Promised Land, 1912 (Excerpts), Mary Antin
- One Family, Two Worlds: an Italian Family's Correspondence across the Atlantic, 1901–1922, (excerpts)
- My China Boyhood (1865–1879), (an excerpt), Chung Kun-Ai
- "One Admonition, Two Admonition", Hakka folksong
- The Effects of Continuous Emigration upon Ireland (1867), John McKane
- The Great Atlantic Migration to North America, Robin Cohen, ed.
- Chinese Indentured Labour: Coolies And Colonies, Ong Jin Hui
- Wanderers or Migrants? Gypsies from eastern to western Europe, 1860-1940, Leo Lucassen and Wim Willems
- The Irish and the "Famine Exodus" of 1847, Robert Scally
- Indentured Migrants From Japan, Mitsuru Shimpo
- The United States Quota Act, 1921–1922 (excerpts)
- Three Bills of Sale for Chinese Prostitutes, An Agreement Paper by the Person Mee Yung
- Chinese Exclusion Act, Approved May 6, 1882
- Regarding the Japanese and Korean Exclusion League, From *Organized Labor*, April 21, 28, and May 5, 1906 [Combined edition]
- An Act to Protect Free White Labor Against Competition with Chinese Coolie Labor, and to Discourage the Immigration of the Chinese into the State of California April 26, 1862
- The People, Respondent, v. George W. Hall, Appellant. Supreme Court of the State of California, 1854.
- The Sand Lot And Kearneyism, by Jerome A. Hart
- Poems of Chinese immigrants to America
- Page Law (Excerpts), March 3, 1875
- Description of Chinese Theater Being Built, *San Francisco Chronicle,* September 25, 1879
- Description of a San Francisco Chinese Funeral, 1903

- Chinese Crowding into Fashionable Districts, *Oakland Herald*, April 28, 1906
- New Chinatown Near Fort Point, Oriental Quarter Removed from Presidio Golf Links at Request of Property Owners, *San Francisco Chronicle*, April 28, 1906
- Chinese Colony at Foot of Van Ness, The Plan to Remove Celestials to San Mateo County Is Opposed, *San Francisco Chronicle*, April 27, 1906
- Chinese Make Strong Protest, *San Francisco Chronicle*, April 30, 1906
- Chinese Housed at Presidio, Later They Will Go to Hunter's Point, *San Francisco Examiner*, April 27, 1906
- The New Chinese Telephone Company, *San Francisco Examiner*, November 17, 1901
- Want Chinese on the Front, May Be Sent East of Telegraph Hill, *San Francisco Examiner*, May 4, 1906
- Issei, Nisei, War Bride: Three Generations of Japanese American Women in Domestic Service (excerpts), Evelyn Nakano Glenn
- The Lebanese in the World: A Century of Emigration, excerpts, Albert Hourani and Nadim Shehadi, eds., First Generation: an 85-year-old Lebanese Entrepeneur in Tucman

SECTION QUESTIONS

- Perspective
    1. What overall pattern or patterns do you notice in the timing of female and whole-family migration?
    2. Are there any events that led to a decline in the number of women and families who migrated?
    3. Are there any events that led to an increase in this type of migration?

MODULE LEVEL QUESTIONS

- What forces were responsible for the large upsurge in global migration from 1840-1920?
- The difference in the number of men and women that migrated from certain countries was often quite pronounced. What (generally speaking) was responsible for such variation?
- Why did a large number of Chinese migrants come to North America in the 19th century and settle in San Francisco?
- What was the function of migration hubs? What common features did they share?
- While the majority of migration between 1840-1920 was voluntary, considerable portions were not -- what migration patterns from this period typically involved the involuntary transportation of people?

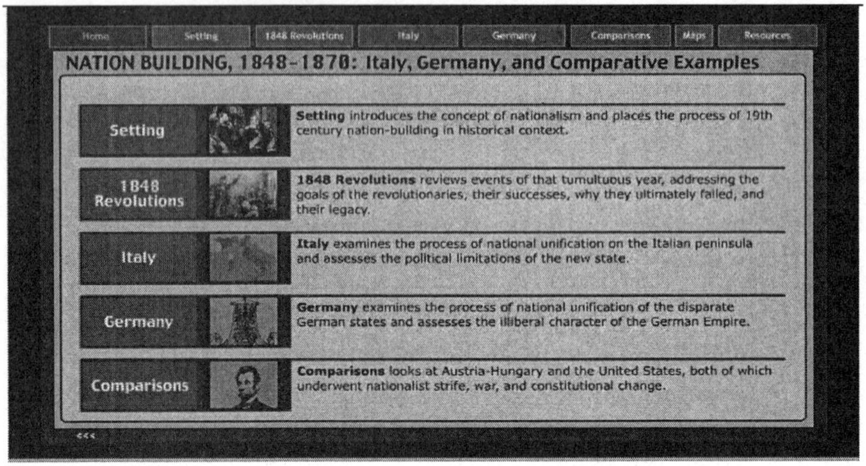

NATION BUILDING, 1848 - 1870: ITALY, GERMANY AND COMPARATIVE EXAMPLES

This module explores nation building in mid-19th century Europe. Beginning with the Revolutions of 1848, it addresses the historical forces shaping and the events leading to the unification of Italy and Germany in the mid-19th century, as well as the limitations of the resulting states. Comparative examples are provided in the form of the Austrian Empire, battered by nationalist pressures from its sundry minority groups, and the United States, rent by war over two divergent social systems.

READINGS:

- Memoirs of Otto von Bismarck (1898)
- Capture of Napoleon III, Otto von Bismark, to his wife, 1870
- Review of Petitti's On Italian Railways (1846), Camillo di Cavour
- On the Origin of Species, Charles Darwin
- Addresses to the German Nation (1808), Johann Gottlieb Fichte
- Frankfurt Constitution of 1849
- Proclamation of the German Empire (1871)
- The Seventh Lincoln-Douglas Debate (October 15, 1858)
- Campaign Manifesto, 1848, Louis Napoleon
- The Communist Manifesto (1848), Karl Marx and Friedrich Engels

- The Eighteenth Brumaire of Louis Napoleon (1852), Parts I and VII, Karl Marx
- The Duties of Man (1844-58), Giuseppe Mazzini
- Metternich Resigns, 1848
- On Liberty (1859), excerpt, John Stuart Mill
- Proclamation by French Government (1848)
- Prussian King Refuses German Crown (1849)
- Social Statics, Chapter II: "The Evanescence of Evil", Herbert Spencer
- Victor Emmanuel's Speech to Parliament (1860)

SECTION QUESTIONS

- Settings
    1. What is meant by social system? What social system do you live in?
    2. Do you discern a relationship between geography/climate and social system?
    3. Think about the role of protective tariffs in the nation building process. Whose interest do they serve?
    4. What are the political implications of social Darwinism within states? Between states?
    5. Do states continue to pursue *Realpolitik* today?
    6. Whom would a centralized, federal political structure benefit? Whom would a confederal political structure benefit?

- 1848 Revolution
    1. In what sense could 1848 be called a "bourgeois revolution"?
    2. Why did the ideologies espoused in the revolutions become particularly acute by 1848?
    3. What was the relationship between nationalism and liberalism before 1848? How did that relationship change as a result of the revolution's failure?
    4. The year 1848 has been called a "turning point at which history failed to turn." Do you agree?

- Italy
    1. Were liberals necessarily anti-clerical?
    2. Why was there hostility between the Church and Italian nationalists?
    3. Why did Cavour fear the success of Garibaldi?
    4. Discuss the following proposition: "the Italian people were not so much the actors of the *Risorgimento* as those acted upon."

- Germany
    1. To what extent were the unifications of Italy and Germany the product of nationalist ideology? To what extent were they the product of statecraft?
    2. What did Bismarck mean by his comment that speeches and majorities were the mistake of 1848-9? What do you think "blood and iron" refer to?
    3. Why did Bismarck introduce universal suffrage?
    4. What conclusions can be drawn from the debate over the constitution in Germany?
    5. Why do you think German national unification failed to fulfill the hopes of European liberals?

- Comparisons
    1. Did the *Ausgleich* help or hinder the Austrian Empire's ability to deal with its nationalities problem?
    2. Was the American Civil War as much about cultural conflict as it was about socio-economic issues?
    3. Is it analytically useful to make historical comparisons among Germany, Italy, Austria and the U.S. in this period?

MODULE LEVEL QUESTIONS

- What are the political implications of social Darwinism within states? Between states?
- What was the relationship between nationalism and liberalism before 1848? How did that relationship change as a result of the revolution's failure?
- Why did Cavour fear the success of Garibaldi?
- What did Bismarck mean by his comment that speeches and majorities were the mistake of 1848-9? What do you think "blood and iron" refer to?
- Was the American Civil War as much about cultural conflict as it was about socio-economic issues?

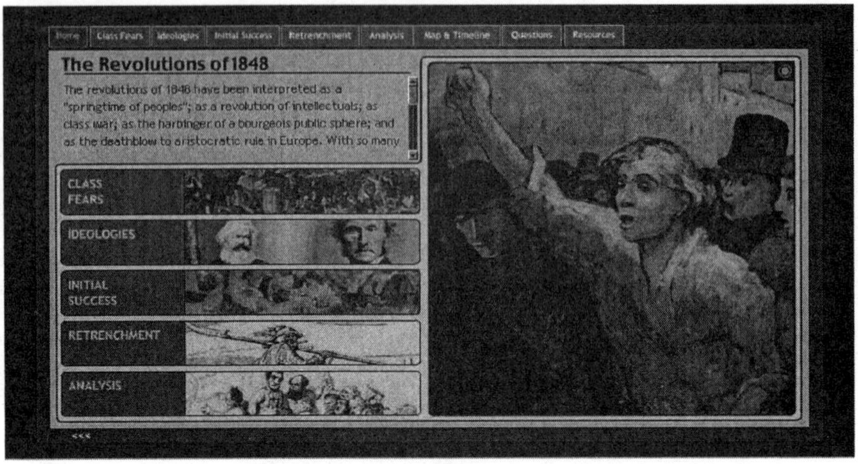

THE REVOLUTIONS OF 1848

This module addresses the Revolutions of 1848 in Europe by i)examining the contending ideologies on the important social issues of the day, around which the conflict revolved; by ii) detailing the events that unfolded over a period of nearly two years; and by iii) providing both a contemporary and scholarly analysis of the revolutions.

READINGS:

- Frankfurt Constitution of 1849
- Campaign Manifesto, 1848, Louis Napoleon
- The Eighteenth Brumaire of Louis Napoleon (1852), Parts I and VII, Karl Marx
- Metternich Resigns, 1848
- Proclamation by French Government (1848)
- Prussian King Refuses German Crown (1849)

MODULE LEVEL QUESTIONS

- In what sense could 1848 be called a "bourgeois revolution"?
- Why did the ideologies espoused in the revolutions become particularly acute by 1848?
- What was the relationship between nationalism and liberalism before 1848? How did that relationship change as a result of the revolution's failure?
- The year 1848 has been called a "turning point at which history failed to turn." Do you agree?

UNIFICATION OF ITALY

This module addresses the unification process of the Italian peninsula in the mid-19th century. It surveys Italy since 1815, while examining different proposals advanced for the form of a new Italian state; the contrasts between North and South; and the role of the Church in Italian political life. Students are then taken through the important aspects of the Risorgimento, including the wars fought with Austria, and the critical involvement of France. Finally, the module takes up the limitations to state building in Italy: the compromises in the South; the characteristics of the new state; and resulting sense of disappointment that beset the peninsula after its creation.

READINGS:

- Review of Petitti's On Italian Railways (1846), Camillo di Cavour
- The Duties of Man (1844-58), Giuseppe Mazzini
- Victor Emmanuel's Speech to Parliament (1860)

MODULE LEVEL QUESTIONS

- Were liberals necessarily anti-clerical?
- Why was there hostility between the Church and Italian nationalists?
- Discuss the role of France in the *Risorgimento*.
- Why did Cavour fear the success of Garibaldi?
- Discuss the following proposition: "the Italian people were not so much the actors of the *Risorgimento* as those acted upon."

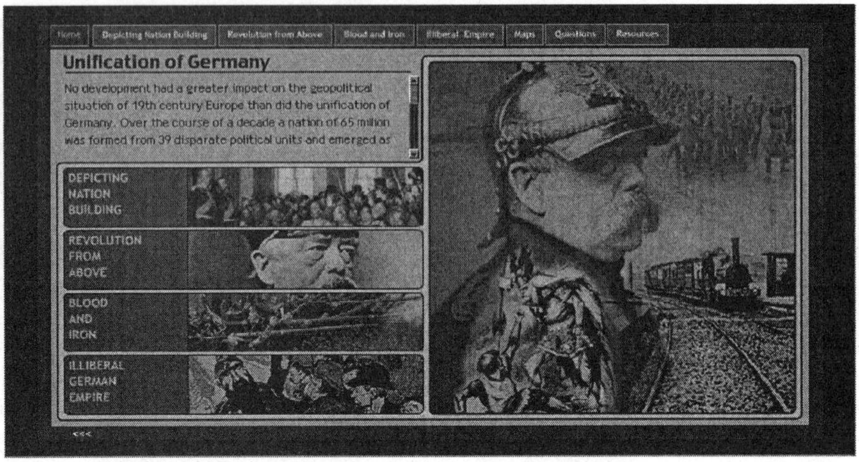

UNIFICATION OF GERMANY

This module covers the process of German Unification; assesses the unique characteristics of German nationalism; examines the social structure of Prussia, under whose auspices Germany was united; looks at the role of Bismarck, together with the notion of "Revolution from Above;" and investigates the illiberal character of the new German Empire.

READINGS:

- Addresses to the German Nation (1808), Johann Gottlieb Fichte
- Memoirs of Otto von Bismarck (1898)
- Capture of Napoleon III, Otto von Bismark, to his wife, 1870
- Proclamation of the German Empire (1871)

MODULE LEVEL QUESTIONS

- What did Bismarck mean by his comment that speeches and majorities were the mistake of 1848-9? What do you think “blood and iron” refer to?
- Why did Bismarck introduce universal suffrage?
- What conclusions can be drawn from the debate over the constitution in Germany?

Why do you think German national unification failed to fulfill the hopes of European liberals?

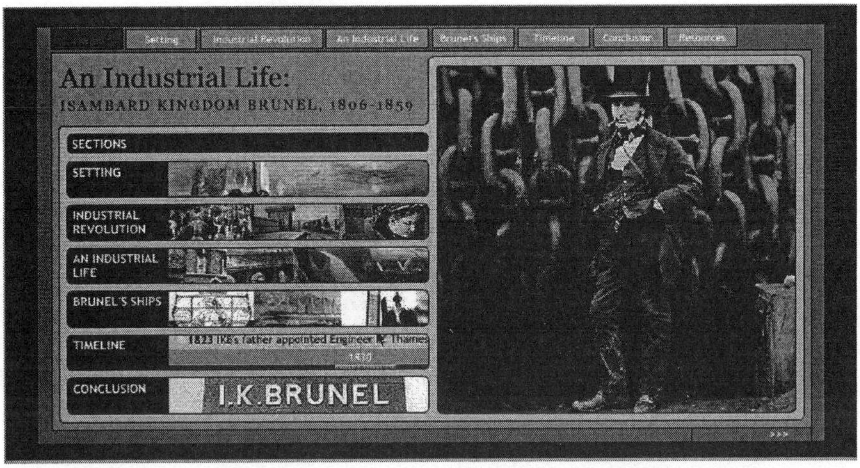

AN INDUSTRIAL LIFE: ISAMBARD KINGDOM BRUNEL, 1806 – 1859

This module explores the major events in the life of the British engineer, Isambard Kingdom Brunel, using both his achievements and failures as a means to better understand the broader themes of the Industrial Revolution in Europe. By studying the life of this important figure in industrial history, the student receives both an engaging biographical narrative and a review of industrial life in Britain during the 19th century.

READINGS:

- The Arrival of the Great Eastern in New York (1860) from Illustrated London News, July 21, 1860
- Diary Entry, February 25, 1854, Isambard Kingdom Brunel
- Diary Entry, December 26, 1835, Isambard Kingdom Brunel
- A letter from a woman on board the Great Britain describing the wreck to a friend in London
- Launch of the Leviathan, from Mechanic's Magazine (December 19, 1857)
- Obituary of Isambard Kingdom Brunel
- Reflections on the Great Britain, Isambard Kingdom Brunel
- Report to Directors of Eastern Steam Navigation Company, June 10, 1852, Isambard Kingdom Brunel

- Report to Directors on the "Management of the Great Ship," October 1855, Isambard Kingdom Brunel
- Report to the Directors of the South Devon Railway Company on August 19, 1844, Isambard Kingdom Brunel

SECTION QUESTIONS

- Industrial Revolution
    1. What are some of the factors that distinguish the earlier Industrial Revolution from the later one?
    2. Does the Industrial Revolution really merit the label "revolution"? Why or why not?
    3. In which general region of Europe did the Industrial Revolution begin? What factors contributed to this?
- An Industrial Life
    1. What role did Brunel's father play in his son's professional life?
    2. What proved so troublesome about the wide-gauge system of rails that Brunel favored? What does this say about the larger process of industrialization?
    3. Why was it thought that a tunnel under the Thames River would be a good idea for London?
    4. Why did Britain's roads, canals, and rails have to expand during the early-19th century?
- Brunel's Ships
    1. What were the innovative features Brunel incorporated into each of his three major passenger steamships?
    2. Why did the Great Eastern eventually come into service laying the transatlantic undersea telegraph cable?
    3. What do the designs proposed by Brunel during the Crimean War have to do with the changing nature of warfare at that time?
- Conclusion
    1. How did the Industrial Revolution change the fabric of Western society in the 19th century?
    2. Which major modern art movements were particularly influenced or otherwise affected by the Industrial Revolution?

Module Level Questions

- When were the "first" and "second" Industrial Revolutions described in the module, and how did they differ?
- Did industrial development occur simultaneously throughout Europe in the 19th century? Why or why not?
- How are the designs that Brunel introduced during the Crimean War indicative of the changing nature of warfare at that time?
- What were some of the cultural repercussions of the Industrial Revolution in Europe?
- To what use was the Great Eastern eventually put?

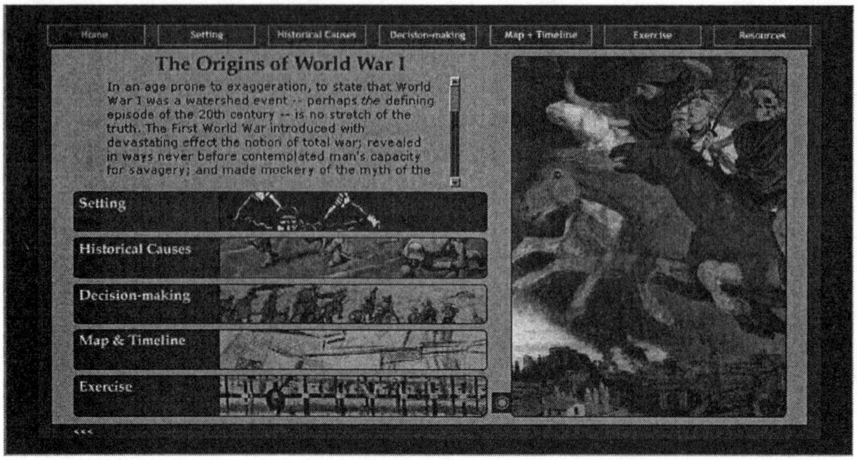

THE ORIGINS OF WORLD WAR I

This module addresses the origins of World War I by examining various historical explanations for the conflict, including both its short-term and long-term causes. By posing a series of questions with accompanying historical evidence, the module puts the student in the role of decision-maker in order to more readily grasp the complexities involved in the run-up to war. An interactive timeline and dynamic map round out the student's understanding of the history and political geography that conditioned decision-making at the time of crisis.

READINGS:

- Samuel Williamson, The Origins of World War I (1988)
- Dual Alliance, October 7, 1879
- Triple Alliance, May 20, 1882
- Russo-German Reinsurance Treaty, June 18, 1887
- Franco-Russian Military Convention (1892)
- Correspondence between France and Britain (1903)
- Entente Cordiale, April 8, 1904
- Anglo-Russian Entente (1907)
- The Tightening of the Entente: Letter of the British Foreign Secretary to the French Ambassador in London, November 22, 1912
- Germany's assurance of support for Austria, July 6, 1914
- Austrian ultimatum; Serbian reply, July 23, 25, 1914
- Kaiser-Tsar Telegrams (10) between July 29, 1914 and August 1, 1914

SECTION QUESTIONS

- Settings
  1. At what juncture during the crisis of the summer of 1914 do you believe European statesmen reached the point of no return?
  2. What role do you attribute to secret diplomacy as a contributing factor for war? Explain.
  3. Describe "the balance of power" concept. How might it have led ineluctably to military conflict?
  4. How real was the threat of social revolution to pre-1914 Europe? Was it simply a pretext for social control by the ruling classes?
  5. Explain relations between the General Staff and the Cabinet (i.e., the government administration). Did these relations assume a different form according to country? How do military-civil authority relations differ today?
  6. To whom do you accord greatest responsibility for the First World War?

MODULE LEVEL QUESTIONS

- What if Serbia had unconditionally accepted all the provisions of the Austrian ultimatum?
- What if Britain had made its involvement in support of Russian and France clear earlier?
- What if Austria-Hungary had acted more quickly in retaliating against Serbia?
- What if Britain and Germany had reached an understanding, or even formal alliance, before 1914?
- What if Britain had not appeased France and Russia on imperial and later continental issues before 1905?

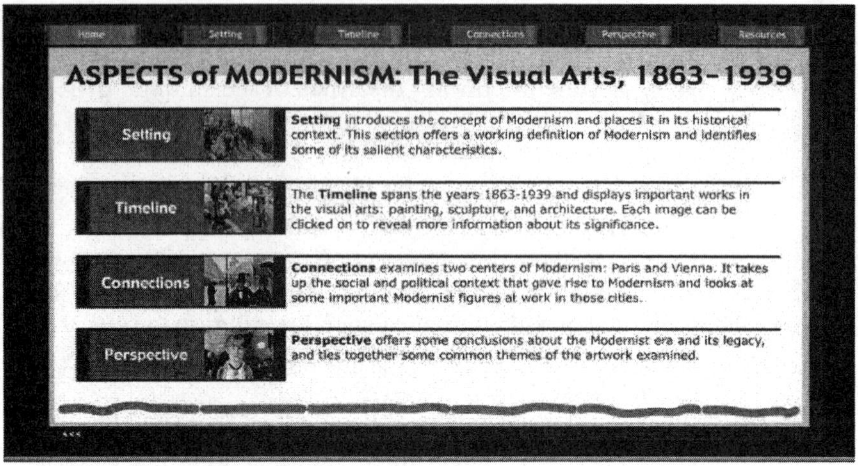

ASPECTS OF MODERNISM: THE VISUAL ARTS, 1863 - 1939

This module introduces the concept of Modernism and places it in its historical context by tethering it to political, social and technological developments of the late 19th and early 20th centuries. The module features a timeline that displays important works in the visual arts -- painting, sculpture and architecture -- and discusses their significance.

READINGS:

- Interpretation of Dreams (1900), Sigmund Freud
- The New Architecture and the Bauhaus, Walter Gropius
- The Founding and Manifesto of Futurism (1909), F.T. Marinetti
- The Future of Architecture, Frank Lloyd Wright

SECTION QUESTIONS

- Settings
    1. Can you think of a cultural event of the last 50 years that may have had the same ability to shock audiences the way Stravinsky's *Rite of Spring* did in 1913?
    2. Why did Modernism emerge when it did?
    3. Discuss Modernism's relationship to the idea of civilization.

- Timeline
    1. Looking at the timeline, which decade would you say was most influential for Modernism and why?
    2. Do you discern common themes among the Modernist paintings?
    3. Are you able to identify any kind of progression in sculpture from Rodin through Boccioni, Brancusi, and Moore?
    4. If you had to devise a modern architectural style, what would be its guiding principles and what building materials would it employ?
- Connections
    1. Compare the late-19th-century Paris and Vienna. What was similar and was what different about these two societies?
    2. Explain the relationship between the city planning and the values of the ruling class.
    3. What gave birth to Modernism in Paris and how was that similar or different from Modernism's genesis in Vienna?
    4. Discuss the proposition, "Klimt was to Vienna what Manet had been to Paris."
- Perspective
    1. What made Manet such an important figure to Modernism?
    2. Discuss Modernism's legacy.
    3. Is Modernism an analytically useful concept?

MODULE LEVEL QUESTIONS

- Do you discern common themes among the paintings representative of Modernism?
- Compare late 19th century Paris and Vienna. What was similar and was what different about these two societies?
- Explain the relationship between city planning and the values of the ruling class.
- What made Manet such an important figure to Modernism? Discuss the proposition, "Klimt was to Vienna what Manet had been to Paris."

EUROPEAN IMPERIALISM 1880 - 1900: THEORY, PRACTICE, DISCOURSE

This module addresses the phenomenon of European imperialism in the late 19th century by first summarizing contending explanations for European imperialism; then by identifying six important interest groups and exploring their relationship to one another, which determined imperialist policies; and finally by examining the operative ideology common to these interest groups, which conditioned the particular form colonization assumed.

READINGS:

- J. A. Hobson, Imperialism: A Study (1902)
- H. P. Anderson: Memorandum, French Occupation of Porto Novo, 11 June 18
- The Berlin Congo Conference: The General Act of Feb. 26, 1885
- Crime of the Congo (1909), Arthur Conan Doyle, 3 chapters
- Heart of Darkness (1901), Joseph Conrad
- Letters from Emin Pasha (1885, 1886)
- Jules Ferry's Foreward to Tonkin and the Motherland (1890), excerpt
- Speech of Former French Premier Jules Ferry to the Chamber of Deputies on July 28, 1885
- King Leopold's Soliloquy (1905), Mark Twain
- Rudyard Kipling, The White Man's Burden (1899)

- Letter from King Leopold II of Belgium to Minister Beernaert on the Congo, July 3, 1890
- E.D. Morel, The Black Man's Burden: The White Man in Africa from the Fifteen Century to World War I (1899)
- Henry Morton Stanley, How I Found Livingstone (1871), excerpts

SECTION QUESTIONS

- Settings
    1. Describe some of the major social, economic and political changes that Europe was undergoing in the late 19th century.
    2. Describe the geo-political situation in the Sudan at the time of the Mahdist rebellion.
    3. Explain the circumstances in which the Emin Pasha Relief Expedition was created. Who had an interest in such an expedition?
    4. Which theory or theories of imperialism do you find most compelling?

MODULE LEVEL QUESTIONS

- What lessons does the Emin Pasha Relief Expedition hold for the phenomenon of imperialism in general? That is, what conclusions can be drawn from it?
- In what ways does the Anglo-German rivalry in East Africa reflect the differing objectives in Africa of Berlin and London?
- Why was the Congo under the personal rule of Leopold II so severely criticized by the international community?
- Describe the ideology at the heart of late 19th century European imperialism and explain how some of the images found in the module reflect that ideology?
- Why did the figure of General Charles Gordon seem to recur throughout the Emin Pasha affair? Who was responsible for invoking this specter and what does this suggest for the influence of media/public opinion at the time?
- Assess the impact on imperialist policy of the various interest groups identified in the module. Did some interest groups wield greater weight than others?

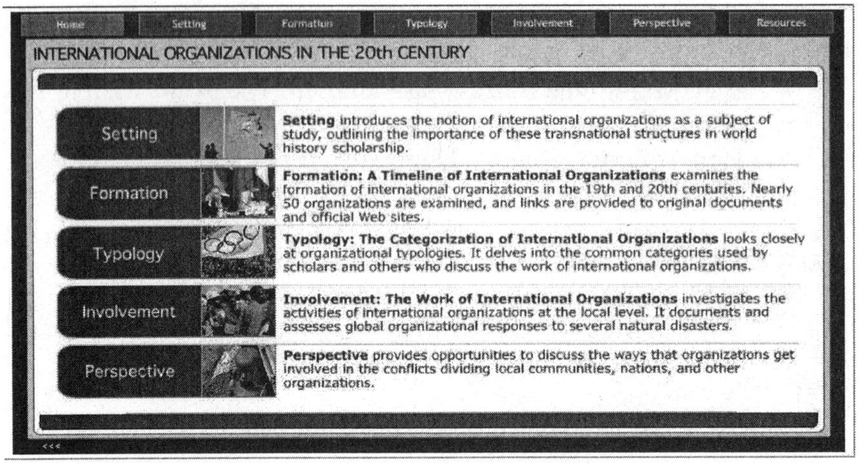

INTERNATIONAL ORGANIZATIONS IN THE 20TH CENTURY

This module examines the formation and interaction of international organizations within world history during the 20th century, communicating the crucial role of these organizations in the modern world community. The history of this period is described as a process - one resulting in benefits as well as problems - by which transnational structures came to be regarded as essential to the workings of the global order.

READINGS:

- A Biography of Henry Dunant (1828-1910)
- 15-Point Program for Implementing Human Rights in International Peace-keeping Operations
- 10 Things You Never Knew About the World Bank
- World Bank Mission Statement
- Charter of the United Nations, Chapter 1
- List of United Nations (UN) Programs
- Preamble to the Charter of the United Nations
- Universal Declaration of Human Rights
- Growth in United Nations Membership, 1945-2000
- Red Cross Main Relief Operations
- Sites of the Olympic Games
- A Memory of Solferino, excerpts
- Restoration of the Olympic Games
- The Fundamental Principles of the Olympic Charter
- The Emblem and the Flag of 1914

- League of Nations Speech, September 25, 1919, excerpts
- League of Nations Membership
- The Covenant of the League of Nations
- Vienna Proclamation
- Amnesty International, Object and Mandate, 1999
- Human Rights Violations from Amnesty International's Annual Report, 2001
- Amnesty International's Appeals for Action

SECTION QUESTIONS

- Typology (Quiz)
  1. Regional defensive intergovernmental organization (IGO)
     North Atlantic Treaty Organization (NATO)
     Warsaw Pact
  2. Regional regulatory intergovernmental organization (IGO)
     Organization of Petroleum Exporting Countries (OPEC)
     Organization of African Unity (OAU)
  3. Global humanitarian intergovernmental organization (IGO)
     UN Food and Agriculture Organization (FAO)
     United Nations Children's Fund (UNICEF)
  4. Global regulatory intergovernmental organization (IGO)
     United Nations
     World Trade Organization (WTO)
  5. Commercial multinational corporation (MNC)
     Nestle
     Standard Oil (later Exxon)
  6. Information/communications multinational corporation (MNC)
     Cable News Network (CNN)
     ITT Corporation
  7. Nongovernmental advocacy organization (NGO)
     International Olympic Committee
     World Wildlife Fund (WWF)

8. Nongovernmental humanitarian organization (NGO)
    Médecins Sans Frontiéres (Doctors Without Borders)
    Save the Children

- Involvement
    1. The case study about the Sahel demonstrates that when many different aid organizations try to make decisions at the same time, the results can be chaotic and unhelpful to victims. Judging from these case studies, who do you think is the ideal agent to manage a crisis? Is it an IGO, an NGO, a government, or the afflicted country itself? Is this the same agent that should make decisions about an afflicted area's needs during a crisis? Why or why not?
    2. In your opinion, what qualities should a relief coordination agency such as the Office for the Coordination of Humanitarian Affairs (OCHA) posses in order to effectively coordinate aid for a crisis such as the Sahelian famine?
    3. The Colombian case study demonstrates the media's importance in times of crisis. What role do you think the media should play at these times? Explain your answer using examples either from this module or from your own knowledge and experience.
    4. When people see media images of disaster victims, it's natural to want their donations to immediately aid those victims. What do you think NGOs can do to educate the public about the need for long-term aid that supplements and sometimes even replaces immediate aid?

5. As shown in the Taiwanese case study, the politics of humanitarian relief can play a positive role (as in the case of Japan) or a negative one (as in the case of China). In your opinion, does politics have any place in the realm of international crisis assistance? If so, how would you define that place? If not, what can be done to reduce the role that it has played?

MODULE LEVEL QUESTIONS

- What four basic functions do international organizations serve?
- What important world event took place shortly before the founding of the majority of the world's international organizations? Why was this the case?
- What categories can you use to help you better understand and differentiate between international organizations?
- One of the main functions of international organizations is to mediate conflicts -- what are the major types of conflicts in which these organizations become involved? Please use examples in your answer.
- Comment on the following statement: "The international news media has become a vital component for fundraising of many international organizations." Do you find this statement essential correct? If so, why or why not?

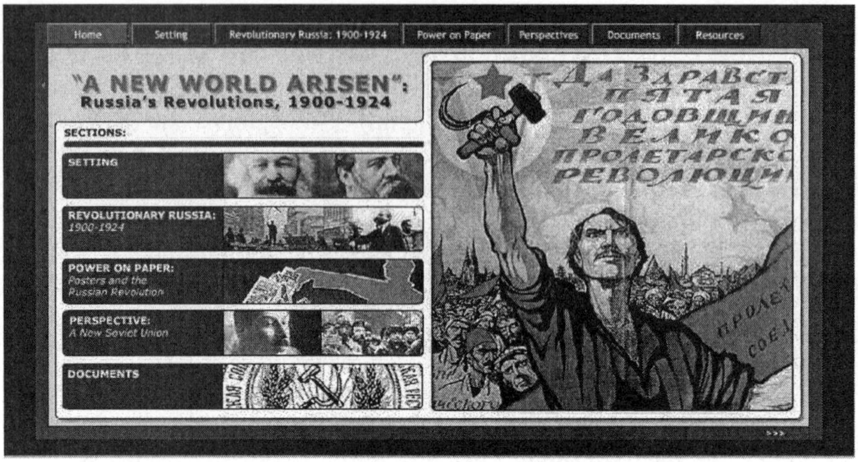

"A NEW WORLD ARISEN": RUSSIA'S REVOLUTIONS, 1900 - 1924

This module explores the period of revolutionary turmoil in Russia from the beginning of the 20th century through the early years of the Soviet Union. The module surveys not only the intense moment of upheaval in 1905 and 1917, but also investigates the background conditions and contingencies that helped shape this quarter century of Russian history. Employing an interactive timeline, maps, images, and primary materials, the module examines not only the patterns of revolution and reaction inside Russia, but also their implications for Europe and the wider world. The module also uses an interactive exercise dealing with Soviet political posters to explore the character of political culture in the new communist regime.

READINGS:

- Allied Decision to Intervene (1918)
- Bolshevik Party Program (1903)
- Nikolai I. Bukharin and Evgenii Preobrazhensky, The ABC of Communism (1920)
- Friedrich Engels, Principles of Communism (1847)
- Fyodor Gladkov, Cement (1924)
- Alexandra Kollontay, The Family and the Soviet State (1918)
- Vladimir Ilyich Ulyanov (Lenin), April Theses (1917)
- Vladimir Ilyich Ulyanov (Lenin), What is to be Done? (1902)
- Manifesto of 17 October 1905
- Comintern Manifesto (1919)

- Appeal to the Moslems (1917)
- Establishment of the Red Army (1918)
- Proclamation of the Assumption of Power by the Soviets (1917)
- George Gapon and Ivan Vasimov, The Petition of the Workers to the Tsar (1905)

SECTION QUESTIONS

- Revolutionary Russia: 1900-1924 (Thought Questions)
    1. What steps defused the Revolution of 1905?
    2. Who was Kornilov and what effect did he have on the Revolution of 1917?
    3. What was NEP? From what you know of the ideological basis for the Revolution of 1917, to what degree do you think this policy was a fulfillment of the radicals' goals?
    4. Why was the set of economic policies known as War Communism replaced with the New Economics Policy in 1921?
    5. What was the "Red Terror" and how did it come about?
    6. What issues divided the Russian Marxists into Bolshevik and Menshevik factions?
    7. How did war function as a catalyst for revolution in Russian history?
- Perspectives (Thought Questions)
    1. Could one argue that the Revolution positively affected the lives of women in the 1920s? If so, how?
    2. How could the formation of the Comintern in 1919 have soured relations between the Bolshevik government and other states around the world?
    3. How deeply do you think the Revolution affected life in remote Russian villages during the early 1920s?

Module Level Questions

- How was the Revolution of 1905 dispersed by the state?
- Briefly explain who the Bolsheviks and Mensheviks were in relation to each other and describe their roles in the cycle of the Russian Revolutions.
- What was the "Red Terror" and how did it come about?
- "Without the experience of war the October Revolution would have died on the vine." Comment on this statement.

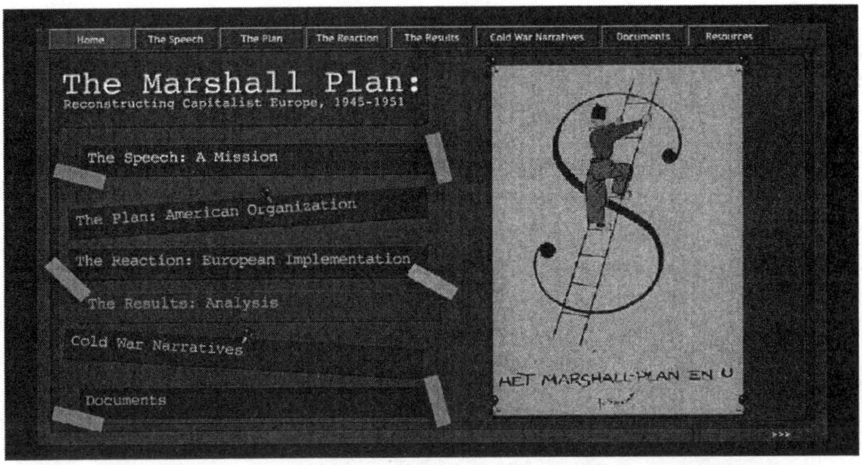

Reconstructing Capitalist Europe, 1945-1960: The Marshall Plan

This module explores the formation, composition, and execution of the European Recovery Program (the "Marshall Plan") launched by the United States following the end of the Second World War. To achieve this , the module employs in-depth document analysis, interactive maps, and exercises to evaluate the conditions of post -war Europe, American planning designed to foster European economic recovery, and European reactions and appropriations in response to the aid program

Readings:

- Morgenthau Plan (1944)
- George C. Marshall, “The Marshall Plan Speech” (June 5, 1947)
- Hoover Report (April 1947)
- Kennan Memorandum (May 16, 1947)
- Clayton Memorandum (May 27, 1947)
- Pravda (June 1947)
- Andrei Vyshinsky Address to UN (September 1947)
- Truman Doctrine (March 12, 1947)
- The Foreign Assistance Act of 1948 (April 3, 1948)
- “Telling the Story of ERP to the Peoples of Western Europe” (August 1949)
- “This is the Road”: Conservative Party General Election Manifesto (1950)

- Labour Party Election Manifesto (1950)
- Paul G. Hoffman, Peace Can be Won (1954)
- Clement Attlee, As It Happened (1954)
- Jean Monnet, "A Method"
- Charles Maier, "The Two Postwar Eras and the Conditions for Stability in Twentieth-Century Western Europe" (1987)

SECTION QUESTIONS

- The Plan (Thought Questions)
    1. What conditions in Europe in 1947 led the United States to invoke the Marshall Plan?
    2. What role did the Office of European Economic Cooperation have in the functioning of Marshall Plan aid?
    3. What was decided at the Potsdam Conference in 1945 and how might this have affected the post-war economic situation in Europe?
    4. What were the basic goals of the Marshall Plan when Congress approved it in 1948?

- The Reaction (Thought Questions)
    1. In what ways did the offer of Marshall Plan assistance affect Eastern European domestic politics? How did this vary from country to country?
    2. Why might Soviet efforts to establish common economic ties in Eastern Europe have been called the "Molotov Plan"?
    3. What was the Monnet Plan and how did it conflict or coincide with the Marshall Plan?
    4. In what ways did British Marshall Plan participation shape the platforms of that nation's Labour and Conservative parties?
    5. What "bargain" did the Italian Prime Minister De Gasperi strike in 1948?

- The Results (Thought Questions)
    1. What meaning is suggested by the statistic that Marshall Plan aid declined as a percentage of a state's national income while that state's production levels rose?
    2. How is the development of the European Coal and Steel Community related to the Marshall Plan?
    3. In what ways could the Marshall Plan be deemed a failure?

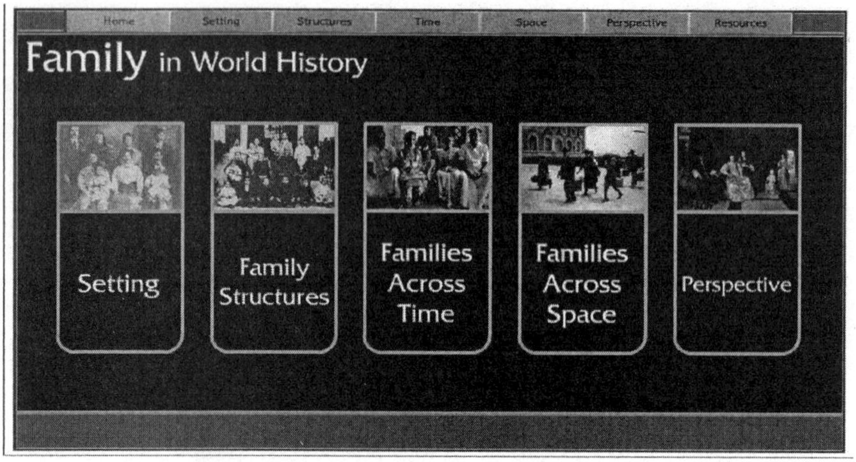

TIES THAT BIND: FAMILY IN 20TH CENTURY WORLD HISTORY
This module closely examines the institutions of family, family practices, rules, and obligations in African, Chinese, Indian, and other cultures in order to understand the role of family structures throughout the world and traces their transformations through time and space.

READINGS:

- Childhood and Family Life under the *Ancien Régime,* Philippe Ariès; trans. Armando Brito
- Sola Family Correspondences, 1901–1922 (Excerpts)
- A Somali Reflects on Life in Toronto
- Three-Generation Story
- Spoken and Unspoken Words in the Life of a Cypriot Woman: A Life Story by Her Granddaughter by Elena Georgiou
- Communication with the Chinese Homeland
- My Daughter Displaced: A Mother's Story, Emily Rishmawi
- An Oral History of a Child Refugee, Vasil Delianov
- My Daughter's Eyes: A Mother/Daughter Story
- A Bend in the River (Excerpts), V. S. Naipaul
- The Ties That Bind: Social Cohesion and the Yucatec Maya Family (Excerpts) Matthew Restall
- Discovering the Invisible Puerto Rican Slave Family: Demographic Evidence from the Eighteenth Century, David M. Stark

SECTION QUESTIONS

- Space
  1. Judging from the examples of these three families in the early 1940s, what were some of the reasons that families migrated to other areas during the first half of the 20th century? Do you think families migrated for the same reasons today? What, if anything, might have changed?
  2. Based on these narratives, what are some of the primary effects of migration on family ties? What does a family potentially lose or gain when its members migrate to other countries?
  3. What were some of the methods that the Satos, Weiszes, and Eliases used to stay in touch with each other? Do you think that staying in touch now is more difficult or less difficult than it was in the 1940s? Why?
  4. From a family's perspective, what seem to be the main problems posed by intermarriage with members of other cultures? In your opinion, do such marriages enrich or erode family cultural traditions? Why?
  5. Using the materials presented in this section, do you think that family migrations from one part of the world to another increase or decrease the possibility of conflict between different generations of a family? Why?
  6. Describe the migratory experiences of your family or a family you know well. Have any of the world-historical events affecting the three families here – for example, war, ethnic or religious oppression, economic depression – had an effect on this family as well? In what ways has this family been changed by its experiences in moving?
  7. Why do you think the formation of diasporic communities is important to the study of world history, and what role do families play in this formation?
- Time ("Thought Questions")
  1. Based on these three examples, what would you say were some of the primary forces of change for traditional family structures during the 20th century? Choose one form of change in particular and explain how it transformed two of the three societies examined.

2. Using the examples of these three families, would you say that the average woman's lot improved or deteriorated over the course of the 20th century? In which of the three societies would you prefer to be a woman? Why?
3. In which society would you prefer to spend your childhood? Why?
4. In some traditionally matrilineal societies, such as the Ashanti in Southern Ghana, the matrilineage has continued to thrive despite the kinds of social changes that have threatened it among the Nayar. Why do you think the family institutions of one society may be more resilient than those of another when faced with the same sorts of cultural pressures? Should local people work to preserve their traditional institutions? If so, how do you think they should do this?
5. Judging from the Chinese, Nuer, and Nayar examples, do you think that governments should legislate family issues? Can you relate the examples here to government legislation in your own society?
6. Some Westerners found the traditional Nayar matrilineal society offensive to western sensibilities, just as some today find China's one-child policy offensive. Keeping in mind both examples, what role do you think outside moral standards should play in any society's decisions on family policy?
7. Using the genealogical models in **Family Structures** and **Families Across Time** as examples, construct two charts for a family in your own society – one circa 1900 and one in the present day. This can be your real family or an imaginary one. Then, use the charts to discuss major changes brought about by economic, political, or social factors during the intervening century.

Module Level Readings

- What are the three general approaches that historians have used to discuss family in world history?
- In what ways have the migration patterns of the 20th century changed basic family structures? Use examples from the module in your answer.
- Using the sample families studied over time in the module as a guide, what would you say are some of the principal ways families have changed since the beginning of the 20th century?
- What is a matrilineal society? Provide at least one example in your answer.
- What subjects does a demographer study? How does this relate to the historical consideration of human family life?